Jim Blank

An IRA Owner's Manual

Your Complete Guide to the Individual Retirement Arrangement

Copyright © 2012 by Jim Blankenship, CFP®, EA

An IRA Owner's Manual

By Jim Blankenship, CFP®, EA

ISBN 978-1468154740 / 1468154745

All rights reserved solely by the author. The author guarantees all contents are original and do not infringe upon the legal rights of any other person or work. No part of this book may be reproduced in any form without the permission of the author. The views expressed in this book are solely the views of the author and do not represent the views of the publisher.

Reproduction or translation of any part of this work beyond that permitted in Section 107 or 108 of the 1976 United States Copyright Act without the permission of the copyright owner is unlawful.

Requests for permission or further information should be directed to the author via email at Jim@BlankenshipFinancial.com.

About the author

Jim Blankenship is a financial planner based in New Berlin, Illinois. Through his Fee-Only financial planning practice, Jim provides unbiased financial advice to individuals from all walks of life.

Jim Blankenship, CFP®, EA

Email: Jim@BlankenshipFinancial.com

★ LINKS

Book: http://IRAOwnersManual.com

Website: http://BlankenshipFinancial.com

Blog: http://FinancialDucksInARow.com

To my darling wife Nan: you mean the world to me.

Acknowledgements

I'd like to thank my friends and colleagues for their help in reviewing, editing and commenting on the drafts of this book. As I've told you all many times, I couldn't do it without you!

In no particular order, my thanks goes out to: Laura Scharr-Bykowsky, Cynthia Petzold, Mike Piper, Josh Giminez, Thomas Horton, Shawn Koch, John Vyge, Steven Young, Steve Ellisor, Buz Livingston, Jim Springer, Lea Ann Knight and Kathleen Campbell. Your contributions to this book have transformed it from my often-incoherent ramblings that amuse only myself, into a useful, reader-friendly guide that (hopefully) will help folks to better understand the IRA.

Thanks so much!

Table of contents

Foreword xi
Introduction xiii
The Basics 1
  General IRA Information 1
    1. History of the Individual Retirement Arrangement 1
    2. IRA Basics 5
    3. Where to Set Up Your IRA 9
    4. The Importance of IRA Custodial Documents 13
    5. Determining Your Modified Adjusted Gross Income (MAGI) ... 15
    6. Comparison and Contrast Between Traditional and Roth IRA 17
    7. Which IRA Is Right For You? Traditional or Roth? 21
    8. Prohibited Transactions Within an IRA 27
    9. Getting the Most Out of Your IRA 29
    10. Creditor Protection for Your IRA 33
    11. Required Minimum Distributions (RMDs) 37
    12. RMD Reporting 41
    13. Roth IRA Eligibility 43
    14. 11 Ways to Fund a Roth IRA 45
    15. Open A Roth IRA for Your Child 49
    16. A SIMPLE Kind of Plan 51
  Rollovers 57
    17. Intro to Rollovers 57
    18. Risk in Rollovers 61
    19. The One-Rollover-Per-Year (OPY) Rule 65
    20. Net Unrealized Appreciation (NUA) 71
    21. Things to Consider Before Rollover 75
    22. Taxes and Rollovers 79
    23. Waivers for the 60-Day Rollover 83
  Roth Conversions 85
    24. Intro to Roth Conversion 85
    25. 5-year Rules 89
    26. Conversion Strategy: Fill out the bracket 95
    27. Conversion Strategy: Remember Social Security 99
    28. Structuring Your Conversion 103
    29. Three Tax-Free Conversions 105
    30. Three Things to Consider 109
    31. Direct Conversion from 401(k) 113
    32. Conversions and the Inherited Plan 115
    33. Conversion Planning for the Small Business Owner .. 117
    34. SGLI Payout Conversion 119
    35. Recharacterization 121

Inherited IRAs **123**
   36. Splitting an Inherited IRA 123
   37. Distribution Period When a Beneficiary is Not Named 125
   38. Disclaiming an Inherited IRA 127
   39. Spousal Inherited IRA 131
   40. Spousal Inherited IRA Rollover 133
   41. The Non-Spouse Beneficiary 137
   42. Problems Arising From Not Taking Timely Distributions 141
   43. IRD From an IRA 147

Special Weapons and Tactics................................. **151**
   Early Withdrawal (72t) Plans.. **151**
   44. Withdraw Retirement Funds Without Penalty (Sec 72t) 151
   45. SOSEPP Distribution Methods 163
   46. One-Time Change to Your SOSEPP 165
   47. Penalties for Changing SOSEPP 167
   48. What Happens When Your IRA Runs Out? 169
   49. How QDRO Impacts SOSEPP 171
   Stretching Your IRA **175**
   50. A Legacy in the Making 175
   51. Mistakes With the Stretch IRA 181
   52. Turn $5,000 a Year Into a $33 Million Legacy 185
   Required Minimum Distributions **189**
   53. RMD (Required Minimum Distributions) 189
   54. Should You Take or Postpone Your First Year's RMD? 193
   55. 5 Tactics for Required Minimum Distributions 195
   Miscellaneous **199**
   56. A Cash Flow Dilemma – Should I Take Distributions From My IRA or a Taxable Account? 199
   57. How QDRO Impacts NUA 201
   58. Turns Out You Can Be a Little Bit Pregnant 205
   59. Using Your IRA to Reduce or Eliminate Quarterly Estimated Tax Payments 209
   60. Deducting IRA Losses 213
   61. The Self-Directed IRA 215

Appendices **219**
   Appendix A 219
   Appendix B 221
   Appendix C 223
   Appendix D 225
   Acronyms 231
   Index 233

Foreword

Together with employer-sponsored retirement plans such as 401(k)s, IRAs are the most important retirement savings tool for investors today.

Unfortunately, like most of the tax code, the Internal Revenue Code sections that provide the rules governing IRAs are obscenely complex. They're simply not made to be understood by normal people, despite the fact that it's normal people – everyday savers and investors – who need to understand what the rules mean so that they can use their IRAs properly.

The IRS does actually provide a series of publications and FAQ-type articles that are fairly understandable. But they're far from comprehensive. And, more importantly, they are entirely lacking any actual advice. That is, they explain the rules, but they leave it up to you to figure out how to apply those rules as part of a tax planning strategy to avoid paying more taxes than you really have to.

Fortunately, there are a handful of people like Mr. Blankenship who actually understand these rules and how to best make use of them, and who care enough to share that information with us.

For the last few years, I've been a reader of Jim's blog (FinancialDucksinaRow.com), and I've found it to be among the most useful personal finance websites I've ever come across. And his recent book <u>A Social Security</u>

Owner's Manual was of a similar caliber. So, naturally, I jumped at the chance to read his work on IRAs. I was not disappointed.

An IRA Owner's Manual is as comprehensive as a book covering such a vast array of interrelated rules could possibly hope to be. It's easy to understand. And most importantly, it provides actionable advice. Throughout the book, Blankenship not only explains the rules governing various IRA-related scenarios, he also makes a point to show you how to navigate the situation to minimize your taxes and avoid costly mistakes.

I hope you find the book as helpful as I have.

Mike Piper, CPA
www.ObliviousInvestor.com

Introduction

As you learn more about your IRA, you may have come to realize, as many have, that it would be mighty useful if all the information about IRAs and retirement plans were in one place. That's a pretty ambitious undertaking – there are literally reams and reams of writings on every type of IRA out there.

I won't pretend that this book contains every piece of information you'll ever need to know about IRAs. So what I've done is to gather within this book many of the common questions people have with regard to IRAs and retirement plans – your own IRA Owner's Manual.

If you're just really interested in the nuances and technical minutiae that surround the IRA, you should start from the beginning and read this manual all the way through. If you're more interested in one or more of the specific topics related either to Roth IRAs or Traditional IRAs, there is a section of the book dedicated to each, as well as to Rollovers and inherited IRAs.

If your primary focus in picking up this book is to discover the more special tricks and strategies you can put into play with your IRA, jump right to the section on Special Weapons and Tactics. As necessary then, once you've read about a particular strategy, you may need to "bone up" on some of the particulars of the law – that's what the earlier chapters can do for you.

I hope you get what you're looking for in this manual, and that I've covered all of the topics that are important to you. If you have questions or comments, feel free to send me an email any time – Jim@BlankenshipFinancial.com.

Happy reading!

jb

The Basics

General IRA Information

1. History of the Individual Retirement Arrangement

In 1974, during the days of Watergate, Hank Aaron's 715th homer, and the oil embargo, Congress passed the Employee Retirement Income Security Act (ERISA) which, among many other provisions, provided for the implementation of the Individual Retirement Arrangement. This original IRA was deductible from income, and the annual contribution limit was the lesser of $1,500 or 15% of household income.

Two primary goals of the IRA were to provide a tax-advantaged retirement plan to employees of businesses which could not otherwise provide a pension plan; as well as to provide a vehicle for preserving tax-deferred status of qualified plan assets at employment termination (rollovers).

The IRA, which was originally offered strictly through banks, become instantly popular with savers, garnering contributions of $1.4 billion in the first year (1975). Contributions continued to rise steadily, amounting to $4.8 billion by 1981.

1978's Revenue Act introduced the Simplified Employee Pension IRA (SEP-IRA), which provided for a contributory retirement account primarily for small businesses. This was the first widely available retirement plan which small businesses could provide for employees in a cost-effective manner.

The Economic Recovery Tax Act (ERTA) of 1981 allowed the IRA to become universally available as a savings incentive to all workers under age 70½. Prior to this point, workers covered by a retirement plan could not participate in an IRA. At the time, the annual contribution limit was also increased to $2,000 or 100% of wage income.

With the passage of the Tax Reform Act of 1986, income limit restrictions were introduced, limiting the availability of deductible contributions to the IRA for individuals with incomes less than $35,000 (single) or $50,000 (Married Filing Jointly) when covered by an employer plan. In addition, provision was made for the Spousal IRA, wherein a non-working spouse could make contributions to an IRA from the working spouse's income, up to $250 annually. Non-deductible contributions were also allowed for those individuals above the income limits, providing tax-deferred growth within the account.

In 1992, provisions were made to the IRA to allow for "special purpose" distributions (known as §72(t) distributions). 72(t) exception distributions are not subject to the 10% early withdrawal penalty. Unless a distribution is eligible for one of the exceptions, a 10% early withdrawal penalty is applied, in addition to ordinary income tax on the distribution.

General IRA Information

1996's Small Business Job Protection Act saw the implementation of the Savings Incentive Match Plan for Employees (SIMPLE IRA), which provided for employer matching and contributions to the employee plans, a viable alternative in many cases to the 401(k), although with more restrictive contribution limits. This act also increased the amount for Spousal IRA contributions from $250 to the annual limit for regular contributions (at the time, $2,000).

With the Taxpayer Relief Act of 1997, the Roth IRA was introduced.

In 2001 came the Economic Growth and Tax Relief Reconciliation Act (EGTRRA), which further increased contribution limits, added a "catch-up" provision for taxpayers age 50 and older, and provided for a nonrefundable credit for certain contributions to IRA and 401(k) plans. These provisions were originally due to expire at the end of 2010, but were extended.

An additional provision in the EGTRRA was the option, available beginning in 2010, for Traditional IRA (TIRA) owners to convert funds to a Roth IRA (RIRA), regardless of income level. Prior to 2010, anyone with an income above $100,000 was ineligible to convert funds from a TIRA to a RIRA. In addition to eliminating the income cap, taxpayers converting Traditional IRAs to Roth IRAs in 2010 were allowed to split taxation evenly on the funds converted between tax years 2011 and 2012. This provision was allowed only in the tax year 2010.

Most recently, the Pension Protection Act of 2006 allowed for charitable giving (free of tax) from an IRA, as well as introducing the Saver's Credit, an income tax credit for lower income individuals, designed to incent retirement saving habits. The Qualified Charitable Distribution (QCD) is set to expire at the end of 2011, but may be extended as it has in the past.

As of this writing in early 2012, the most recent data from the Investment Company Institute indicates nearly 40% of all Americans own an IRA account, and the accounts held approximately $4.9 trillion of retirement funds.

2. IRA Basics

To start off, let's discuss the basics of IRAs. The following information holds true for both Traditional IRA (TIRA) and Roth IRA (RIRA) plans.

IRA accounts can be held at a variety of institutions, from banks and credit unions to brokerages and insurance companies. Essentially, if it is a financial institution, quite likely there is an IRA offering. Typically, an account is established by filling out an application, identifying yourself by name, address, and Social Security number. You'll be asked to name a beneficiary – a decision not to be taken lightly, but we'll get to that issue a bit later. Having filled out the necessary paperwork, you will send off the application, along with your contribution to the account. Often this entire action can be done online, although a paper application often needs to be sent afterwards to satisfy the beneficiary documentation requirements.

Eligibility for a Traditional IRA

Following are the eligibility requirements for a Traditional IRA:

- You must have earned income. This means you have received compensation in the form of wages, salaries, tips, professional fees, bonuses, commissions, self-employment income, nontaxable combat pay, and/or taxable alimony or maintenance.

- If you are eligible for and covered by a retirement plan in your workplace (even if you don't participate), in order for the IRA contributions to be deductible from your income, your Modified Adjusted Gross Income (MAGI) must be less than:

    o $112,000 (for 2012) if your filing status is Married Filing Jointly or Qualifying Widow(er) (phased out* beginning at $92,000); or

    o $68,000 (for 2012) if your filing status is Single, Head of Household, or Married Filing Separately (and you did not live with your spouse at any time during the year) (phased out* beginning at $58,000); or

    o $10,000 if your filing status is Married Filing Separately and you lived with your spouse at any time during the year.

- If you are not covered by a retirement plan from your employer, there is no limit to your income. You're eligible to contribute to a deductible IRA up to the limit for the year. *It should be noted the term "covered by a retirement plan" means a retirement plan is available to you and you are eligible to participate – regardless of whether or not you actually participate.*

- If you are covered by a retirement plan from your employer and your income is above the limits listed above, you can still make non-deductible contributions to a Traditional IRA, up to the annual limit.

In any given year, there is a limit to the amount you are allowed to contribute to ALL IRAs. This means the total

General IRA Information

of all of your contributions, whether to a TIRA or a RIRA, cannot exceed the annual limit ($5,000 for 2012, see www.IRAOwnersManual.com for the current year's limits). If you are age 50 or older, there is an additional "catch-up" contribution allowed. The catch-up contribution amount is $1,000 for 2012.

It is important to understand the term "Individual" in Individual Retirement Arrangement is taken quite literally: IRAs are Individual instruments, not jointly held, so the limits mentioned above (except for MAGI) are per individual, not per household.

There are household income limits which apply in some cases, which we'll cover in Chapter 5.

* The term "phased out" refers to the fact that deductibility becomes gradually reduced between the MAGI amounts of $92,000 and $112,000 for married filing jointly. Given the deductible limit for 2012 is $5,000, for each dollar that your MAGI is greater $92,000 the deductible limit is reduced by 25% (or 30% if you're over age 50), rounded up to the nearest $10. If your MAGI is less than the upper limit but the calculation here results in less than $200, you are allowed to deduct at least $200.

For single or Head of Household filers, the phaseout for deductibility is between MAGI amounts of $58,000 to $68,000, at a 50% rate for each dollar over the lower limit (60% if over age 50). Just like before, if the result is less than $200 and your MAGI is less than the upper limit, you are allowed to deduct at least $200.

An IRA Owner's Manual

3. Where to Set Up Your IRA

Establishing and contributing to an IRA (Traditional or Roth) is pretty simple and straightforward. Banks, savings and loans, credit unions, insurance companies, mutual fund companies, and brokerages all offer IRA accounts. There are pros and cons to each type of institution, as we'll list below. These alternatives represent the major options for opening your IRA, in no particular order.

Banks, Savings and Loans & Credit Unions

Pros: Banks are thought to be the most stable and conservative institutions in our financial industry. For many folks, this is an assurance of additional safety in placing funds with these institutions. And in a way, with FDIC insurance, there is additional safety.

Cons: Since banks are typically conservative, until recently their options for investment of IRA funds were somewhat limited. Traditionally, cash-oriented investments such as CDs and Money Market Accounts were the primary means of investment within banks. This has changed lately with deregulation, as many banks now offer mutual fund investments in addition to the traditional offerings. By this deregulation, banks are now in a similar position to brokerages, selling products on commission.

Insurance Companies

Pros: While there are many arguments about the merit (or lack thereof) to placing annuity investments into IRAs, this is the primary option insurance companies bring to the table. Annuity investments can provide a stable guaranteed income stream for retirement.

Cons: The investment options insurance companies offer tend to be limited and expensive by comparison to other options since the focus is on annuity products. Far more cost-effective options can be found in other choices of where to keep your account. Annual expense ratios for annuities typically run in the 2+% plus range, for example. In addition to the costs, annuities charge a fee (called a surrender charge) if you cash in the contract within a specified number of years. These charges often can "lock up" your funds for up to fifteen years for some annuities.

Mutual Fund Companies

Pros: Typically the lowest-cost provider of IRAs, with a wide variety of investment offerings. In addition, once the account is established, at many mutual fund companies there are no transaction costs for additional contributions. This supports the concept of dollar-cost-averaging*.

Cons: Many mutual funds have minimum investment levels, making investment into the funds difficult within an IRA, especially in the early years of the account. In addition, with the exception of no-load mutual funds, typically there are sales charges associated with the funds, ranging anywhere from 2% up to 5% and more. These sales charges can be assessed at the front end (when you buy the fund), or the back end (when you sell), or may be assessed annually while you own the fund.

General IRA Information

Brokerages

Pros: Generally the widest variety of investment choices. Depending upon the brokerage, can be a very cost effective option, in terms of transaction costs.

Cons: Brokerages typically have a transaction cost with each contribution, which can make dollar-cost-averaging* costly. Each individual contribution, if invested immediately, can generate a transaction fee ranging from $10 to $50, depending upon the brokerage. Discount brokerages don't offer much assistance, but that may be a positive: the "full-service" brokerages tend to push their own proprietary funds or investments paying the broker a better commission.

* * * * * * * * * * * * * * * * *

As you can see, there are positives and negatives to each type of institution. You need to be comfortable with your choice of financial institution for your IRA, as you will potentially be dealing with the company for many years into the future. Although you could make a change (transfer your funds) to a different institution at pretty much any time within limits, making those changes can be a hassle, so it's best to be very comfortable with your choice up front.

I mentioned the term "dollar-cost-averaging" a few times in the preceeding paragraphs, so I thought it might help to provide a definition:

Dollar-cost-averaging is a shorthand description of a strategy for investing wherein you invest the same amount of money on a regular interval, such as monthly or every payday. Each interval, you purchase the same investment — such as a mutual fund. As the price of the fund varies over time, on the increases in price you'll purchase fewer shares, but on the decreases in price you'll purchase more shares, since you're always using the same dollar amount each interval. This is how most 401(k) and similar plans' investments work. If you are investing from current income over longer periods of time, this method is your default.

There have been many studies to determine if this method is beneficial versus a lump-sum investment (if you have the lump sum available). It's generally agreed, lump-sum investing is at least as good if not better than the gradual dollar-cost averaging method. However, if there is a cost associated with each purchase, dollar-cost-averaging can be an expensive method for investing.

4. The Importance of IRA Custodial Documents

Remember when you opened your IRA account? And the broker or advisor handed you a 37-page document with the custodial agreement in it? The little "book" written on cigarette paper? I'll bet you read the whole thing cover-to-cover, dintcha?

Unfortunately, too many of us don't read these documents closely, and we may end up getting a big surprise later on. "What sorts of surprise?", you might ask. Well, here are two major surprises which could await you:

Per Capita or Per Stirpes? If you have multiple beneficiaries of your IRA, this will be important to know – because it's up to the custodial document to determine how your account will be distributed. Here's why – Per Capita means, for example, if you have three equal beneficiaries designated on your account and one of the beneficiaries pre-deceases you, the account will then be split in two, between the two remaining beneficiaries. If the account were to be split Per Stirpes, the two remaining beneficiaries would still each receive a 1/3 share, and the beneficiaries of the deceased beneficiary would receive the remaining 1/3 share. Typically there is a check-box on the beneficiary form to help you designate your beneficiaries as you wish, but ultimately the control comes down to the custodial document. This becomes even more important with the second consideration.

Divorced, but forgot to change beneficiary form? Depending upon the custodial agreement, the custodian

What happens if the former spouse is the only named beneficiary on the account, and the former spouse pre-deceases the account owner? could follow the court's ruling, wherein the divorce decree declares all property to be split as indicated and named in the document, with no other splitting to be done; or, the custodian could go strictly "by the book", where the beneficiary form indicates a specific individual as the primary beneficiary, regardless of any other outside document. And here is how the Per Stirpes/Per Capita issue becomes important in this case: what happens if the former spouse is the only named beneficiary on the account (no secondary beneficiary(s)), and the former spouse pre-deceases the account owner? If the custodian holds to the Per Stirpes definition, the former spouse's heirs could reap the benefits of the account… scary huh?

So, in the end, it pays to know a little about the custodial documents on your IRA account, just so you don't have any surprises. If you don't understand it or can't follow what the document is telling you, make your advisor explain it to you — especially these two factors mentioned above. It's part of an advisor's job — to advise you — and you're paying the advisor for advice.

5. Determining Your Modified Adjusted Gross Income (MAGI)

The IRS has placed limits by filing status for deductibility if you are covered by an employer-provided retirement plan. Your filing status and your Modified Adjusted Gross Income (MAGI) are important factors in setting the limits of deductibility for TIRAs. In addition, the MAGI is used to determine a taxpayer's eligibility to make regular contributions to a Roth IRA.

In order to fully understand these limitations, you need to understand what makes up your Modified AGI (MAGI). The MAGI is calculated as follows:

1. Start with your Adjusted Gross Income from line 38, Form 1040, or line 22, Form 1040A.
2. Add back your IRA deduction amount from line 32 on Form 1040 or line 17 on Form 1040A.
3. Add back your student loan interest from line 33 on Form 1040 or line 18 on Form 1040.
4. Add back any tuition and fees deductions from line 34 on Form 1040 or line 19 on Form 1040.
5. Add any domestic production activities from line 35 on Form 1040 (there is no line for this on 1040A).
6. Add back any foreign earned income exclusions from line 18 of Form 2555EZ or line 45 of Form 2555.
7. Add back any foreign housing deduction from line 50 of Form 2555
8. Add back any excluded qualified savings bond interest shown on line 3, Schedule 1, Form 1040A, or line 3, Schedule B, Form 1040 (from line 14, Form 8815)
9. Add back any excluded employer-provided adoption benefits shown on line 30, Form 8839.

The total of these nine items listed above makes up your Modified Adjusted Gross Income, or MAGI.

See Appendix D for the MAGI limitations for the various filing statuses for tax year 2012. You can find each current year's MAGI limitations and other useful updates at the website www.IRAOwnersManual.com.

6. Comparison and Contrast Between Traditional and Roth IRA

What's the difference between the two types of IRAs? And what is similar?

You probably know a little bit about this subject – like one IRA is deductible on your income taxes, and the other one has *some* kind of tax benefit. But the differences are hard to understand, and can be even harder to explain! Below are the major differences between the two, followed by the similarities. This discussion is liable to be useful as you consider which kind of IRA is best for you (and both could be best for you, at different times in your life).

Differences Between Traditional IRA and Roth IRA

Deductibility is a feature of the Traditional IRA (TIRA) which is not available in the Roth IRA (RIRA). What this means is, subject to the MAGI limits discussed in chapter 5, you may be able to deduct the amount of your annual contribution to your TIRA from your income, in the year of the contribution. This is one of the primary reasons TIRAs have remained as popular as they are to this day. At the time of the introduction of the IRA, very few companies offered 401(k) plans, so the TIRA offered one of the only tax sheltered savings opportunities available to many taxpayers.

Tax treament is another major difference between the two kinds of IRA. The TIRA's distributions are always taxable (if the distribution is not a rollover or made up of non-deducted contributions) as ordinary income, while the RIRA's distributions are always tax-free (as long as they meet the requirements, such as after age 59½). What is also very different about the two is your *contributions* to a RIRA are always available for withdrawal at any time for any reason – tax free. The growth in the RIRA (interest, dividends and capital gains) would be taxed and subject to penalty if withdrawn for an ineligible reason prior to age 59½. The TIRA does not have a provision allowing withdrawal of your contributions tax- and penalty-free at any age.

The TIRA has Required Minimum Distributions (RMD), while the RIRA has no requirement for distribution.

Required distributions are the final major difference covered here. The TIRA has Required Minimum Distributions (RMD) which must begin once the owner reaches age 70½, while the RIRA has no requirement for distribution during the life of the original owner. In other words, the Roth IRA never needs to be distributed during the IRA owner's life, while the Traditional IRA must be distributed beginning at the owner's age 70½.

Similarities Between Traditional IRA and Roth IRA

Income requirement. A requirement of both the TIRA and the RIRA is the holder (or the holder's spouse) must have *earned income* in the year of the contributions. The income must be at least equal to the total of all IRA contributions for the year. This includes two additional types of contributions: spousal contributions and non-deductible contributions.

General IRA Information

Spousal contributions are allowed for both the TIRA and the RIRA. The spousal contribution essentially allows a spouse with income to contribute to the IRA (either variety) in the name of the spouse who either does not have income, or whose income is below the maximum available contribution for the tax year. The total IRA contributions are limited, however, to the total of both spouses' *earned income* for the tax year.

Earned income, for the purposes of IRA contributions, includes wages, salaries, tips, commissions, self-employment income, or alimony (or separate maintenance payments). Not included as earned income are: earnings and profits from property (rental or royalty), interest income, dividends, pensions, annuities, deferred compensation (such as 401(k) distributions), certain non-participatory partnership income, and capital gains.

Non-deductible contributions to a Traditional IRA are allowable at any income level. In essence, if your income is too high to make either a RIRA contribution or a deductible TIRA contribution, you are allowed to make a non-deductible contribution of up to the maximum amount allowable for the year into your TIRA. These contributions are *after tax*, and so when distributed there will only be tax on the growth which has occurred in the account. Non-deductible contributions are a way to defer tax on the growth of funds in an account. Non-deductible contributions are also available as a spousal contribution. As a matter of practice, if you are making non-deductible contributions to an IRA, it can be helpful in the long run if you establish a separate IRA account to segregate non-deductible contributions from other IRA funds. More on this later.

Tax Year Specification. TIRA and RIRA contributions must be made for a specific tax year. In other words, since there are strict limits on the contribution amounts each year, you must specify the tax year of the contribution to your IRA. You are generally allowed to contribute for a tax year beginning on January 1 and ending on the tax due date for the year (generally April 15 of the following year). In other words for 2012 you may make your contribution to your IRA at any time between January 1, 2012 and April 16, 2013.

The same time limit applies to establishing the account as well. You can even file your tax return early, indicating a contribution to your TIRA (and deducting it from your gross income) before you make the contribution! Just make sure you do go ahead and make the contribution... the IRS has very little sense of humor about things like this!

Penalty for withdrawal applies to ineligible distributions from either type of account. A 10% penalty will be applied to any distribution from an IRA of either variety which is not specifically allowed under §72(t) (see Chapter 44 for more information on 72(t) distributions), above and beyond the ordinary tax applied to the distribution.

7. Which IRA Is Right For You? Traditional or Roth?

For retirement savings in general, there is a recommended "Order of Contributions". The order is as follows:

1. Contribute enough to your employer-provided retirement plan to get the company matching funds.

2. Maximize your contribution to a Roth IRA.

3. Continue increasing your contribution to your employer-provided plan up to the annual maximum.

Beyond those three items, you may want to consider college savings accounts, tax-efficient mutual funds in a taxable account, or a low-cost annuity, among other choices.

However, the question at hand here is this: Which is better, a Roth IRA or a Traditional IRA?

The answer, as usual, is a fully-qualified "It depends". I'll explain the most important factors below.

If you were to consider the two types of accounts side-by-side, at first glance you'd think it doesn't make any difference which one you contribute to – especially if you assume the tax rate will be the same in retirement (or distribution phase) as it was before retirement (or accumulation phase). This is because you're paying the same tax on the distribution of the Traditional IRA after the investment period, simply delayed, as you paid on the Roth contribution, only this part is paid up-front.

Clear as mud, right? Let's look at the following table to illustrate. I have purposely not included any increases in value, as we'll get to that a bit later. In the example, we're using a 20% ordinary income tax rate.

Year	Roth	Tax	Trad	Tax
1	$1,000	$250	$1,250	$0
2	$2,000	$500	$2,500	$0
...				
10	$10,000	$2,500	$12,500	$2,500

Each year we had $1,250 available to contribute to either a Traditional or a Roth. We had to pay tax on the Roth contribution each year, but we were able to make the whole contribution, tax-deducted, in our Traditional account.

What happens when we throw growth into the account? The following table reflects the next step in our analysis, with each account growing at 10% per year, and the values are as of the end of the year:

Year	Roth	Tax	Trad	Tax
1	$1,100	$250	$1,375	$0
2	$2,310	$500	$2,888	$0
...				
10	$17,531	$2,500	$21,914	$4,383

If you subtract the tax from the Traditional balance, you come up with the same number as the Roth account, since there is no tax on the Roth account at distribution. Although you pay more in taxes, you had more

General IRA Information

contributions to your account, so it all comes out in the wash.

So far, there isn't any compelling evidence indicating whether you should use a Roth instead of a Traditional IRA. Let's make another change to the table, by assuming the tax rate in distribution is 25%, and we remain at a 20% rate during accumulation. The following results come from this change:

Year	Roth	Tax	Trad	Tax
1	$1,000	$250	$1,250	$0
2	$2,310	$500	$2,888	$0
...				
10	$17,531	$2,500	$21,914	$5,478

As you can see, this results in a nearly $1,100 increase in taxes at distribution, making the Roth IRA the preferred option. Conversely, if the ordinary income tax rate is lower in distribution, the Traditional IRA is a better option.

There are some other factors we could consider and run calculations on, but for the most part we've covered the important bases.

By strictly running the numbers, the Roth IRA is preferred when the income tax rate is higher in retirement, and it's at least as good as the Traditional IRA if the rates remain the same. If the numbers were the only differences between the two accounts, this is not a strong argument for the Roth, because you're just making a gamble as to what will happen with tax rates in the future.

Thankfully, there are more factors to bear on the decision. Below I list three very good reasons to choose a Roth IRA over a Traditional (deductible) IRA.

Three Very Good Reasons to Choose The Roth IRA Over the Trad IRA

1. Roth IRA proceeds (when you are eligible to withdraw them, at or after age 59½) are tax free. That's right, there is no tax on the contributions you put into the account and no tax on the earnings of the account. You paid tax on the contributions when you earned them, so in actuality there is no additional tax on these monies.

2. There is no Required Minimum Distribution (RMD) rule for the Roth IRA. With the Trad IRA, at age 70½ you must begin withdrawing funds from the account, whether you need them or not. For some folks, this could be the biggest benefit of all with the Roth IRA.

3. Funds contributed to your Roth IRA may be withdrawn at any time, for any reason, with no tax or penalty. Note that this only applies to annual contributions, not converted funds, and not the earnings on the funds. But the point is, you have access to your contributions as a sort of "emergency fund of last resort". While this benefit could work against your long-term goals, it may come in handy at some point in the future.

4. (a bonus!) A Roth IRA provides a method to maximize the money you pass along to your heirs: Since there's never a tax on withdrawals, even by your heirs, the amount of money you have in your Roth IRA is passed on in full to your beneficiaries, without income

taxation to reduce the amount they will eventually receive – estate tax could still apply though.

As illustrated, if you believe ordinary income tax rates will remain the same or increase in the future, the calculations work in favor of the Roth IRA.

With those factors in mind, and given that most folks have a generally pessimistic view of tax rate futures in the US, the Roth IRA seems to be the better choice in nearly all situations.

Note: We continue discussing Roth IRAs in Chapter 13.

8. Prohibited Transactions Within an IRA

In an IRA account you have a wide range of investment choices, typically only limited by the custodian's available investment options. There are, though, specifically prohibited investing activities for IRA funds.

What's Not Allowed for IRA Accounts?

Self-Dealing. You are not allowed to make investments in property which benefits you or another disqualified person. A disqualified person includes your fiduciary advisor and any member of your family, whether an ancestor, spouse, lineal descendant (child) or spouse of a lineal descendant. It is important to note that this limit applies to both present and future use of a property – so if you purchased a condo (for example) and rented it out exclusively for several years and then decided to convert it to personal use, this act would disqualify the investment and potentially classify it as a distribution, to be taxed and possibly penalized (with interest) retroactively.

Borrowing. You are not allowed to borrow funds from your IRA account. Likewise, you are not allowed to put up your IRA account as collateral for a loan.

Selling/Buying. You are not allowed to personally sell property to or buy property from your IRA account.

Collectibles. Collectibles are the single specific class of investments you cannot invest in with your IRA. This includes art, antiques, gems, coins, and alcoholic beverages, among other items. There is an exception to the coin prohibition: you are allowed to invest in one, one-half, one-quarter, or one-tenth ounce U.S. gold coins, or one-ounce silver coins minted by the Treasury Department with your IRA funds. You can also invest in certain platinum coins and certain gold, silver, palladium, and platinum bullion.

Unreasonable Management Costs. It is prohibited to pay an exorbitant amount to an advisor to manage your account. It IS an allowed transaction to pay your advisor, tax-free, from your IRA *specifically for managing the IRA account.* However, if the fee amount is deemed unreasonable (e.g., obviously for services above and beyond managing the IRA account), this transaction is prohibited.

Life Insurance. You may not purchase life insurance contracts with your IRA account funds. It is permissible though, to own an annuity contract with a death benefit rider within your IRA.

Beyond these transactions, IRAs have a pretty wide scope of available investment options, as I indicated before, mostly limited by the custodian's available investments. In cases where the IRA funds are to be used for more complex investments, such as individual real estate transactions, a special custodian is often required. These transactions can be very difficult to complete and manage over time and maintain the tax-qualified status, so a qualified custodian can be very valuable. See Chapter 61 for more details on Self-Directed IRAs.

9. Getting the Most Out of Your IRA

Most all of us have at least one IRA account, and often we have a couple of accounts, including a Roth IRA and the Traditional IRA (or "Trad" IRA).

The rules for these accounts can become quite complex, especially as we begin drawing funds out of the accounts or considering what will happen with the account at our demise, but we shouldn't let the complexities keep us from using IRAs. The benefits from using IRAs can be huge – and you should use the rules of the IRAs to your advantage in order to wring every bit of value from the accounts. In this chapter, we'll review three of these important factors.

Start Early

As with nearly every other facet of financial planning, time is a huge factor in the favor of building up your net worth. I often recommend parents encourage their children to contribute to an IRA as soon as the child begins earning money (see Chapter 15). Starting an IRA early and allowing the magic of compounding to work for you will allow you to grow a significant fund over your lifetime. The more time you have your contributions in the account, the more time for the money to grow, tax deferred.

Choose Between a Roth IRA and a Traditional IRA for Annual Contributions

This topic alone could cover many pages (see Chapter 7 for a complete discussion), but the gist of it is this: if you are able to deduct the IRA from your income and you are in the 15% tax bracket or higher, you should first consider contributing to a Trad IRA. This is because of the tax-deductible nature of contributions to these accounts. In nearly every other case, it makes more sense to make your annual contributions to a Roth IRA.

Here are three very good reasons for choosing the Roth IRA over the non-deductible IRA (or a deductible IRA if your income allows). I listed these in chapter 7, but they are important enough to repeat:

1. Roth IRA proceeds (when you are eligible to withdraw them, post age 59½) are tax free. That's right, there is no tax on the contributions you put into the account and no tax on the earnings of the Roth IRA account. You paid tax on the contributions when you earned them, so there is no additional tax on these monies or the growth on your investments.

2. There is no Required Minimum Distribution (RMD) rule for the Roth IRA. With the Trad IRA, at age 70½, you must begin withdrawing funds from the account, whether you need them or not. For some folks, this is probably the biggest benefit of all with the Roth IRA. This way you can pass along a larger fund to your heirs, tax free.

General IRA Information

3. Funds contributed to your Roth IRA may be withdrawn at any time, for any reason, with no tax or penalty. *Note: this only applies to regular annual contributions, not to converted funds, and furthermore does not apply to the earnings on the funds.* But the point is that you have access to your contributions as a sort of "emergency fund of last resort". While this benefit could work against your long-term goals, it may come in handy at some point in the future.

Roth IRA funds can be an "emergency fund of last resort" for you.

Choose the Right Beneficiary Option

By choosing the beneficiary(ies) with your overall estate plan in mind, you and your heirs can effectively stretch out the benefits of your IRA for significant periods of time (see Chapter 52 for an illustrated example). Since taxes are not due on the account's holdings until they are withdrawn, delaying withdrawal for the longest period of time makes a great deal of sense. There are many complicated nuances to assigning beneficiaries to your IRAs, and your overall estate planning goals need to be considered.

Your spouse (as beneficiary) will be able to treat your IRA as his or her own and use his or her own life as the determining factor in RMD calculations. In the case where the surviving spouse is significantly younger, this can have a dramatic positive effect in the "stretching" of an IRA (more about the Stretch IRA in Chapter 48).

If you choose instead to direct your IRA proceeds to your children or grandchildren, it often makes the most sense to ensure that each child is designated as the primary, sole beneficiary on a separate IRA. Otherwise, there are a lot of moves to be made in order for each beneficiary to have control over his or her portion of the account. In addition, make sure your heirs understand the impact of inheriting an IRA. Without proper knowledge, an unwitting heir might trigger a huge tax cost to utilize an inherited IRA on today's wants, rather than tomorrow's needs.

Plan Which Investments to Hold in Your IRA

Given the tax-deferred nature of Trad IRAs and the tax-free nature of Roth IRAs, it makes good sense to place specific components of your overall portfolio's asset allocation into these accounts. This sort of planning is most flexible when you have taxable holdings in addition to your IRAs and qualified retirement plans, such as a 401(k) or deferred compensation plan.

Income-generating assets such as bonds or dividend-paying mutual funds should be placed in these deferred accounts, deferring (or avoiding) taxation to a later date. Appreciating assets, like most growth stock funds, should be placed in taxable accounts (or better yet, Roth IRA accounts), since the capital gains taxes are lower than the income tax rates as of this writing. To quote a colleague of mine, Laura Scharr-Bykowsky: "Tax location is every bit as important as tax allocation" – meaning from the tax perspective, what type of account you put various funds into is just as important as the types of assets you're investing in.

10. Creditor Protection for Your IRA

In this day and age with bankruptcies quite commonplace, often this question comes up: are my retirement plan assets protected from creditors? And there are two ways you can take this – are the assets protected from creditors of my employer; and are the assets protected from my personal creditors?

Employer Creditors

Your qualified retirement plans (401(k), 403(b), etc.) are always protected from creditors of your company, against the event your company should declare bankruptcy, for example. The same is true for traditional qualified pension plans. However, with certain nonqualified retirement plans, there is a strong possibility these assets could be accessed by your employer's creditors in the event of a bankruptcy.

These plans are often called executive compensation, rabbi trust, deferred compensation, or supplemental retirement savings (among many other terms). The key here is these accounts are "non-qualified", and as such are not protected by the ERISA law. These accounts are very often open to access by creditors, so be aware of this if you're a participant in such an account. Check with your HR department if you're unsure if your retirement account(s) are qualified (and thus protected by ERISA) or not.

IRAs, being individual accounts totally separate from your employer (unless you're self-employed) are not considered in any way the assets of your employer. If you are self-employed and are not incorporated in some fashion, some of your IRA assets could be at risk, depending upon the state you live in and the balance of the account (see below).

Personal Creditors

In general, the Bankruptcy Abuse Prevention and Consumer Protection Act of 2005 (BAPCPA) provides that both Traditional and Roth IRAs derived from contributions are protected from creditors up to $1 million. This protection only applies to bankruptcy, not to other judgments, and as such state law applies for all other situations. The level of creditor protection varies widely by state. For more up-to-date information on the protection within your state, see the website www.assetprotectionbook.com. Rollovers from employer plans, including trustee-to-trustee transfers (see Chapter 18 for more detail), SEP or SIMPLE IRAs have *unlimited* protection from creditors, due to ERISA law.

The level of creditor protection for IRAs varies widely by state.

In a case decided in 2007 in Kansas, an inherited IRA with a *revocable* trust as the beneficiary became available to the decedent's creditors. (Other states may have differing laws, this was just an example.) The way to resolve or avoid this situation is to use an *irrevocable* trust as the beneficiary and use discretionary and spendthrift clauses within the trust as protection. Otherwise, naming an

34

individual (or individuals) as the IRA beneficiary(ies) would avoid this problem as well.

Further problems develop in the inherited IRA spectrum due to the fact that most state courts do not consider an inherited IRA to be a "retirement account", since the owner (the beneficiary of the decedent) is currently receiving an income from the account. This is important because *retirement accounts* are specifically protected from creditors (due to BAPCPA).

Conclusion

So, even though the IRA has somewhat fewer protections against creditors compared with employer plans, if you've left the employer this shouldn't be the reason to leave funds in the old account. An IRA account can be considerably more flexible, easier to access, and (likely) lower in cost overall. If protection against creditors is a great concern, umbrella liability and/or malpractice insurance could be used as a low-cost alternative.

11. Required Minimum Distributions (RMDs)

As you are likely well aware, once you reach age 70½ you're required to begin taking minimum distributions from your IRA and/or qualified retirement plans each year. There are several things you need to know about these distributions, so you don't make any mistakes. Listed below are some of the more important rules – but keep in mind these Required Minimum Distribution (RMD) rules are only for the original owner of the account, not for a beneficiary of an inherited account. *There are separate rules for an inherited account, which you'll find information about beginning in Chapter 36.*

Calculation of RMD

1. You must have your account balance from the end of the calendar year prior to the year for which the distribution is being calculated. Any additions or withdrawals *after* December 31 of the previous year are not included in this balance, even if an addition is for the previous calendar year. Also, any "in flight" rollovers or recharacterizations that effectively would impact the end of year balance are included (or excluded) in the balance as applicable.

2. You must learn your distribution period, which can be found in Table III (see appendix C), using your age at the end of the current year (not the previous year).

3. Divide the balance from #1 by the distribution period found in #2. This is your RMD for the current year.

4. For each subsequent year, go back through #1 for a new balance at the end of the prior year, then go to the table from #2 to get a new distribution period, and do the math.

Example

Let's work through an example of RMD calculation. John is 70½ this year, and he has an IRA that had a balance of $100,000 at the end of the previous year. According to Table III, with an age of 71 at the end of this calendar year, the distribution period factor is 26.5. Dividing $100,000 by 26.5 yields a result of $3,778.53 – this is the minimum distribution John must take for this calendar year. Since it's his first year, John can delay this distribution to as late as April 1 of the following year.

More Than Minimum – for any year in which you withdraw more than the RMD amount you are NOT allowed a credit against future year RMD. The result is your balance at the end of the current year is lower, so future RMDs are also lower as a result, but not by the amount of extra distribution you received.

No Rollovers or Conversions of RMD Amounts – Although you're allowed to rollover or convert IRA funds after age 70½, you cannot rollover or convert the *amount attributable to your RMD* for the year.

Multiple Accounts – For the purposes of calculating RMD, the IRS *considers all Traditional IRAs owned by one individual as one aggregated IRA.* This means you can determine your RMD by adding

Start the RMD calculation by adding together the balances of all your Trad IRA accounts...

together the balances of all your Trad IRA accounts at the end of the prior year, and then taking your RMD from any one account (or as many accounts as you wish) as long as it totals at least the RMD for the year. Other qualified retirement plans such as a 401(k) must be treated separately – that is, the RMD must be calculated only on the specific account and the distribution received from only that account.

Multiple Payments – You are allowed to take from as few as one payment to as many payments as you wish from your IRAs, as long as the payments add up to at least the RMD for the year.

12. RMD Reporting

So we've talked about how to determine your Required Minimum Distributions (RMD) from your IRA and when you must take it. How does the IRS know you've done what you're supposed to? As you might expect, the IRS doesn't leave such things to chance.

Any time you receive a distribution from an IRA, a Form 1099-R is generated. If this is for your RMD for the year (considered as a normal distribution) there will be a Code of 7 in Box 7 of the form. This will be true of any amount you receive from your IRA in a "normal" distribution. The amount of the distribution will be found in Box 1 of the form, and the taxable amount will be in Box 2.

In addition, a Form 5498 will be generated for your IRA and sent to you by January 31 of the following year – meaning, if you receive a Form 5498 before January 31 of the current year, it is relating to an IRA balance as of December 31 of the prior year. This statement will either detail the amount of your RMD (based on your age, the standard table, and the balance in the IRA as of 12/31) or may include an offer to calculate the RMD amount if you request.

Both of these forms are filed with the IRS as well, so they'll know if you've made the appropriate distributions from your plan(s).

13. Roth IRA Eligibility

The Roth IRA represents a very valuable retirement savings vehicle. There are several reasons the Roth IRA is so valuable, including:

- qualified withdrawals are tax free

- withdrawal of regular contributions is available at any time for any reason

- there is never a Required Minimum Distribution for the original account owner

With all of these benefits, you can see why the Roth IRA has become a very popular option for retirement savings. So the question now becomes: Am I eligible to contribute to a Roth IRA?

Roth IRA Eligibility

The eligibility requirements for a Roth IRA are as follows:

- You must have earned income. This means you have received compensation in the form of wages, salaries, tips, professional fees, bonuses, commissions, self-employment income, nontaxable combat pay, and/or taxable alimony or maintenance.

- Your Modified Adjusted Gross Income (MAGI) must be less than:

o $183,000 (for 2012) if your filing status is Married Filing Jointly or Qualifying Widow(er); or

o $125,000 (for 2012) if your filing status is Single, Head of Household, or Married Filing Separately (and you did not live with your spouse at any time during the year); or

o $10,000 if your filing status is Married Filing Separately and you lived with your spouse at any time during the year.

And that's it. You are not limited by participation in an employer-sponsored plan as you are with deductibility of a Traditional IRA. There are a few additional limiting factors, though:

- You cannot contribute more than your earned income.

- A spousal contribution is allowed, as long as the total of contributions to personal and spousal IRAs doesn't exceed the total of your personal and your spouse's combined earnTd income.

- You are limited by an annual amount (for 2012 it's $5,000 with a $1,000 "catch-up" contribution if you're over age 50). In other words, your total IRA contributions (Traditional and Roth added together) cannot exceed the annual limit.

You can see Chapter 5 for more details on the MAGI limits and how they are applied.

14. 11 Ways to Fund a Roth IRA

With due regards to Natalie Choate of the law firm Nutter McClennen & Fish LLP for initially putting this list together, below are the currently-legal methods for funding a Roth IRA account:

1. Contributions from compensation income. These are your regular annual contributions to the Roth IRA account. You are allowed (in 2012) to contribute up to the lesser of your actual earned income compensation or $5,000 – provided your Modified Adjusted Gross Income (MAGI) is below the limits (see www.IRAOwnersManual.com for current year limits).

2. Catch up contributions. If you are over age 50 during the tax year, you are eligible to make an additional contribution of $1,000 (for 2012) above and beyond the "regular" contributions. This figure is reduced if your compensation income for the year is less than the total of the regular contribution plus the catch up contribution for the year.

3. Conversion from a Traditional IRA. This is a special sort of taxable rollover from your Traditional IRA account to a Roth IRA account. Ordinary income taxes are owed on the amount converted – but no penalty will be applied to all monies converted successfully from The traditional IRA to the Roth IRA. *Note: If the Traditional IRA is composed of both deductible and non-deductible contributions, the conversion taxation can become*

45

very complicated. See Chapter 58 for more details on how this works.

4. Conversion from a Qualified Retirement Plan such as a 401(k). Much the same as #3 above, you may be eligible to convert funds from your QRP to a Roth IRA account. See Chapter 31 for more details on how to accomplish this type of conversion.

5. Rollover from a Roth 401(k). If you have a Roth 401(k) through your employer, with plan-specific limits you may be eligible to rollover the funds from the Roth 401(k) to your Roth IRA. Your own contributions to the account plus the growth can be rolled over tax-free to the Roth IRA account. There are no income limits on such conversions; however there can be limits on when you would have access to the rolled-over funds, depending upon your age at the time of the rollover, the age of the accounts, and other factors.

6. Rollover from an inherited Qualified Retirement Plan (QRP). As detailed in Chapter 32, if you've inherited a Qualified Retirement Plan you could be eligible to convert those funds to a Roth IRA.

7. Failed rollovers or conversions. If you have attempted to make a rollover or a conversion into your Roth IRA and for some reason it is disallowed – such as you inadvertently had a higher MAGI (Modified Adjusted Gross Income) than anticipated – the amount contributed to the account (if not recharacterized) will be considered a regular contribution, subject to the following tax consequences:

General IRA Information

a. a 6% excise tax per year for any excess contribution not removed from the account

b. the distributions from the Traditional IRA or QRP (if a conversion) must be included in your gross income

c. the distributions will be subject to the additional 10% penalty for an early distribution not covered by an exception, conversion or rollover

8. Certain military death benefits. As a result of the HEART Act, certain payments of Servicemember's Group Life Insurance (SGLI) benefits can be rolled over into a Roth IRA with no tax or penalty. Chapter 34 provides more details.

9. Qualified reservist distributions. A member of any of the US military reserves who has received compensation during active duty is eligible to place those funds in a Roth IRA at any time during the two years *following* active duty, without regard to normal contribution limits.

10. Exxon Valdez settlements. Certain individuals who received settlement compensation in connection with the Exxon Valdez oil spill can contribute up to $100,000 of the settlement into a Roth IRA without regard to normal contribution limits. Individuals include both the original plaintiffs and the heirs of the original plaintiffs. To be eligible for this contribution, the settlement would be claimed as income in the year received, and the contribution must be made during the same tax year as it is claimed as income.

11. Certain payments to employees of bankrupt airlines. Within 180 days of receipt of payments made in connection with bankruptcy of an airline, these payments or a portion of the payments, can be contributed to a Roth IRA without regard to regular limitations.

Note: #10 and #11 have some fairly narrow requirements; you can find more about these in IRS Publication 590.

15. Open A Roth IRA for Your Child

Here's a very good idea to consider – if you have a teenager who has a part-time job, rather than putting those earnings solely into a savings account (or worse, a car), open a Roth IRA. The money contributed to this account will mostly be tax free, since the first $5,950 (2012 figures) of earned income is not taxed for a single filer who is a dependent of another.

Since contributions to the Roth IRA are "after tax", the first $5,000 of income earned (for 2012) and the future earnings on that income *will never be taxed* if contributed to a Roth IRA. And since as a parent you're paying for most everything else the child needs anyhow, why not encourage him to make a contribution of his first $5,000 of income into a Roth IRA?

One downside (or maybe it's an upside?) to this strategy is that the contributions will be available (without tax or penalty) for college expenses, down payment on a home, or whatever. However, if the money is left in the account it can provide a tax-free source of income for retirement in the future. This can be a good time to introduce the concept of saving for something far into the future to your child.

An added benefit of putting the money into a Roth IRA account is that money in retirement accounts (such as a Roth IRA) will not be included in the FAFSA calculations for student financial aid. If this money was put into a savings account, the savings account would be counted as a source of funds to pay for college expenses (on the FAFSA).

Money in retirement accounts is not included in FAFSA calculations for financial aid.

If Junior begins a job mowing lawns at the age of 12, earning $2,000 per year until he's age 18, if he contributed all of his earnings to a Roth IRA and the account earned 5% per year, he could have an account worth more than $16,000 by the time he is ready for college – and it wouldn't be counted against his financial aid calculations. If he was able to leave the funds alone, with no other contributions he could have an account worth more than $115,000 by the time he reaches retirement age!

Two key factors to remember are:

- The child must have earned the income. This means the income was reported to them on a W2 or 1099, or possibly the child was self-employed. The income must be reported on an income tax return in order to account for the income, even if no tax was owed on the earnings. (*Note: don't get carried away with this idea and "invent" income for your child. Allowance for mowing the yard or cleaning her room does not generally count as income. Some folks might disagree with my view on this but I don't believe it's wise to push the law to the limit.*)

- The Roth IRA contribution must be made before the regular due date of the tax return for the year in question. For the 2012 tax year, for example, the contribution to the Roth account must generally be made by April 16, 2013.

16. A SIMPLE Kind of Plan

The SIMPLE Plan is a type of retirement account for small businesses that is simpler (ah hah!) to administer and more portable than the 401(k) plans which are common in larger businesses. SIMPLE is an acronym (probably a backronym, more likely) which stands for Savings Incentive Match PLan for Employees.

A SIMPLE Plan can be either a part of a 401(k) plan, or using IRAs – and what we'll cover is primarily the IRA-type of SIMPLE plan. The difference is, there are more restrictions on employer activities, and less room for error (as can be the case with 401(k) plans).

A SIMPLE Kind of Plan

Much like a 401(k) plan, a SIMPLE Plan is an agreement between the employer and employee wherein the employee agrees to a salary deferral. This deferral effectively reduces the employee's take home pay, and the employer then agrees to contribute the deferred amount into the SIMPLE IRA account on behalf of the employee. These contributions must be made to a SIMPLE IRA account, not a Traditional IRA.

To be eligible for a SIMPLE Plan, the employee must have received at least $5,000 in compensation during any two years prior to the current tax year, and can reasonably expect to receive at least $5,000 in compensation in the current tax year (calendar year). For the purposes of the SIMPLE Plan, a self-employed individual would be considered an employee if she received *earned income* as described. Also, certain classes of employees can be excluded from participation, such as union members subject to collective bargaining, or nonresident aliens who have received no compensation from US sources.

Types of Contributions

There are three different types of contributions that can be made to a SIMPLE Plan – salary deferrals, employer matches, and nonelective contributions.

Salary Deferrals are much the same as 401(k) salary deferrals. The employee decides to defer a percentage of his salary, which reduces his taxable and take-home pay, and the deferral is contributed to a SIMPLE IRA on his behalf.

Employer Matches are also similar to the equivalent activity in a 401(k) plan. The employer elects to match the employee contributions, dollar-for-dollar, up to 3% of the employee's salary, although this amount can be less. (see *Limits below for additional information*)

Nonelective Contributions - in some cases, the employer may decide to make contributions on behalf of ALL eligible employees, rather than only for those who are participating in the SIMPLE Plan. In this case, the employer has opted for making the Nonelective Contributions instead of Employer Matching Contributions. These Nonelective Contributions are for 2% of employee salary.

Limits

For Employer Matching contributions, the employer has some leeway in making the contributions for a particular tax year, but there are quite a few restrictions on how this leeway can be applied:

- as described above, the matching contribution must be dollar-for-dollar, up to 3% of the employee's deferral for the year; however -

- the matching contribution can be reduced to as little as 1% (or any amount between 1% and 3%) for a tax year as long as the amount is not reduced below 3% for more than two out of five tax years (including the current tax year) and the employees are informed in a timely fashion of the reduction in match.

- the Nonelective Contribution of 2% can be substituted for the Employer Matching Contribution for any given year as long as employees are notified.

Contributions (for 2012) are limited to $11,500 in employee deferrals, plus a catch up provision of $2,500 if the employee is age 50 or older during the tax year. Employer matches are limited to the amount the employee defers, up to 3% of compensation.

Note: a SIMPLE deferral is counted toward the overall 401(k) limit ($17,000 for 2012) in deferrals for the tax year. If an employee is elibible for more than one retirement plan, this limit applies to all deferrals for the tax year. SIMPLE deferrals do not count toward your IRA contribution limits though.

Additional thoughts

There are a few additional things of interest regarding rollovers and the SIMPLE plan to list:

- You are not allowed to rollover or transfer funds from a Traditional IRA into a SIMPLE IRA. If this is done by mistake, you can recharacterize those funds back into a Trad IRA (see Chapter 35 for more information on recharacterizations).

- In order to rollover amounts from your SIMPLE IRA into a Traditional IRA (any type of IRA, including SEP-IRA), the account must have been in existence for at least two years; otherwise your only option for a rollover is into another SIMPLE IRA (which then inherits the earlier SIMPLE IRAs starting date for rollover purposes).

- The same two-year rule applies to converting a SIMPLE IRA to a Roth IRA. In other words, the SIMPLE IRA must have been in existence for two years before you can convert the account to a Roth IRA.

- Early distributions (not subject to any of the exceptions) which occur during the first two years of the account's existence are subject to a 25% additional penalty (instead of the usual 10% penalty for other IRA accounts).

Other than those restrictions, all of the other distribution rules apply to SIMPLE IRAs as apply to Traditional IRAs:

General IRA Information

- distributions are taxable as ordinary income; with some exceptions, qualified distributions can not begin until age 59½;

- rollovers and trustee-to-trustee transfers are allowed as non-taxable events (subject to the two year rule above);

- conversions to Roth IRAs are allowed without penalty (subject to the two-year rule); and

- early distributions not subject to exception are subject to an additional 10% penalty (25% in the first two years as described above).

Rollovers

17. Intro to Rollovers

Conventional wisdom says: when you leave a job, whether you've been "downsized" or you've just decided to take the leap, you should always move your retirement plan to an IRA. *(Note: when referring to "retirement plans" in this book, the plan could be a 401(k) plan, a 403(b), a 457, or any other qualified savings deferral-type plan).*

But there are a few instances when it makes sense to leave the money in the former employer's plan.

You have several options of what to do with the money in your former employer's plan, such as leaving it, rolling it over into a new employer's plan, rolling it over to an IRA, or just taking the cash.

The last option is the worst. You'll automatically lose 10% via penalty from the IRS (unless you meet one of the exceptions, including first home purchase, healthcare costs, and a few others) if you're under age 59½, plus you're taxed on the funds as if it were income. For the highest bracket, this can amount to losing as much as 45% of the account.

In addition, if you think about it, by cashing out you're derailing the retirement fund you've put so much effort into setting aside. If you cash it out, you've got to start over, and you've got less time to build the account back up. A 2005 change in the tax law requires your old employer to automatically roll over your account into an

IRA if it is between $1,000 and $5,000 (if you don't choose another option), to keep folks from cashing out. If your account balance is more than $5,000, the old employer is required to maintain your account in the old plan until you choose what you're going to do with it.

With recent tax law changes, another option has become available for your old account: you can now roll these funds over into a new employer's retirement plan, as long as the new employer's plan allows it. In many cases this may make good sense, especially if the new plan has good investment choices and is cost-effective.

If the new plan doesn't suit you, you can always roll the funds from your old employer's plan into an IRA. You'll then be able to decide just how you want to allocate the investments, choosing from the entire universe of available investment options, rather than the limited list many employer plans have available. Caution is necessary when doing this type of rollover, as a misstep could cause the IRS to treat your attempted rollover as a complete distribution, having the same tax effect as cashing out. Seek the help of a professional if you are unsure about how to deal with this situation.

But when would you leave the funds at the old employer? If the old employer's plan is a well-managed, low-cost plan, and you're happy with how your investments have done, then you might just want to leave the money where it is. In addition, if you happen to be over age 55, you may have options available to access the funds immediately, rather than waiting until age 59½ – but only if you leave the funds in the original employer's plan. Plus, if your plan is a 457 plan (generally only available to federal, state or local governmental employees), you may be able to tap the plan upon your ending employment (at any age) without penalty as well.

Another good reason to leave the fund at the old employer is if you believe there is a high probability you may return to this employer. Especially in the case of working for a government agency, it may make sense to leave those funds in the applicable plan when you think there is a better than average possibility you might return to work with the government (even another agency), as there are benefits available in the plan that you would be giving up if you moved your account to an IRA, and you're not likely to be able to move those funds back when you return.

... if you happen to be over age 55, you may have options available to access the funds in your 401(k) plan immediately, rather than waiting until age 59½...

An IRA Owner's Manual

18. Risk in Rollovers

The idea of an IRA rollover, or a rollover IRA, isn't necessarily a cosmic mystery – this happens all the time. You leave your job, and you rollover your 401(k) to an IRA. No problem, right? Unfortunately, there often are problems with the process of moving funds from one account to another – because there are a couple of very restrictive rules regarding how this process can and cannot be done. It's not terribly complex, but you'd be surprised how easily these rules can trip you up.

Rollover Risk

Let's start with a few definitions:

A **Rollover** is when you take a distribution from one qualified plan or IRA custodian, *in the form of a check made out to you*, and then you re-deposit the check into another qualified plan or IRA account (at a different custodian). The restrictions on a true rollover from one IRA to another IRA are:

- the deposit into the new account must be made no more than 60 days after the distribution from the old custodian; and

- a rollover can only be done once every 365 days (and yes, 366 days if February 29th is included!).

There are exceptions to the "once-per-year" (OPY) rule, such as: this only applies to IRA-to-IRA rollovers. Rollovers to or from an employer plan, either to or from an IRA or another employer plan, are not subject to the OPY rule. Also, Roth conversion is not subject to the OPY.

The only exception I know of with regard to the 60-day rule is if the rollover amount becomes frozen (due to bank insolvency, for example) during the 60-day period, and therefore cannot be withdrawn and sent to the new custodian. If this situation occurs, the IRA account owner must complete the rollover within 10 days after the deposit is no longer frozen.

Now, in the case of a medical issue which keeps the IRA account owner from completing the rollover, it is possible to petition the IRS for a waiver of the 60-day rule, and given appropriate circumstances these are almost automatic.

It is also important to note that the OPY rule applies separately to each IRA. (see Chapter 19 for more on the OPY rule.)

A **Trustee-to-Trustee Transfer (TTT)**, even though it is often referred to as a "direct rollover", is treated differently from the Rollover (described above). These transfers, being from one custodian to another (the money never gets into the taxpayer's hands) are instantaneous transfers, so the 60-day rule has no bearing on it. Also, the TTT is not restricted to the OPY rule.

Why is this so important? When would you make more than one rollover in a year? One case might be where you were waiting for maturity of certain instruments in one IRA (like a CD, for example) and through the course of less than a year, you had two CDs come due and you took rollover distribution from each in separate checks. The second (and any subsequent) rollover from the same account in the 12 month period would be disallowed and considered a taxable (and most likely penalized) distribution.

Two more rules on rollovers

In addition, the TTT helps to avoid any issues with another rule on rollovers: you are required to rollover the **same property** that was distributed. This means the IRA account owner cannot receive cash as a distribution and then rollover stock shares which he's purchased with the cash. Likewise, you couldn't receive shares of stock in one company, sell the shares and purchase stock in another company and rollover the new shares. One exception to this rule is if you receive stock from a company plan (like a 401(k)), you can sell the stock and rollover the cash into an IRA.

If one of those transactions occurs, your rollover funds are considered excess contributions above and beyond the annual limit and you would be subject to 6% excess accumulation tax for each year the funds were in the account, on top of being taxed on the original distribution, and quite likely penalized as well.

> The last rule I have to offer is this: a **non-spouse beneficiary** can never do a 60-day rollover; they must always do a TTT – as any check written to a non-spouse beneficiary is considered a taxable distribution, and there is no relief available if this mistake is made.

So a good rule of thumb is this: unless there is a very compelling reason, you should always go with a Trustee-to-Trustee transfer when rolling funds to an IRA – this way you'll avoid some very unpleasant results. If you have to do the other kind of rollover – make sure you haven't done another within a year and you'll be golden.

19. The One-Rollover-Per-Year (OPY) Rule

As mentioned in the previous chapter, there is a strict rule the IRS applies with regard to IRA rollovers: you are allowed to roll funds over from an IRA using the 60-day rule only once during each 12-month period. *FYI: Trustee-to-Trustee transfers are not considered rollovers for this rule.*

Here's an example of what could happen: Early in the year, Jane withdraws some money from her IRA to help catch up on some bills. Then, she receives a bonus a little later in the year, within the 60-day period from her withdrawal, so she deposited those funds back into the same IRA.

Then, later in the year, Jane wants to take another short-term distribution from her IRA, and once again she has the opportunity to put the funds back into the first IRA… but now she's stuck. She can't roll the distribution back into the original IRA, since it's still within the 12-month period, and it won't be up until after her current 60 days is passsed. And she can't roll it into another IRA either, since the rule applies to the IRA from whence the funds were rolled out.

Here's what you can do

There are two main choices in a situation such as the one above:

1) Rollover the IRA money into a qualified plan, such as a 401(k) or 403(b). Not all of these plans allow "roll-ins" but many are beginning to allow them. The 12-month rule

doesn't apply to rollovers from an IRA to these other types of plans.

2) Convert the funds to a Roth IRA. Even though you'll have to pay tax on the conversion, this can be a valid move as well. The 12-month rule also doesn't apply to conversions. Plus (and here's the sneaky part) if you wanted to recharacterize the Roth conversion, you could place the converted funds back in the original IRA, even if it was still within the 12-month period. This is due to the fact that a recharacterization is NOT considered a rollover for the purpose of the one-rollover-per-12-month rule.

Heartaches Caused By the OPY Rule

There is no way, procedurally, for the IRS to grant an exception for the OPY rule.

One of the big reasons why this rule can cause so much heartache is because there is no way, procedurally, for the IRS to grant an exception, no matter what the circumstances are. For example, in the 60-day-rollover rule, often the IRS may be in a position to grant an exception, especially if something awful happened to make you miss the deadline. This sort of exception is not even a consideration for the One-Rollover-Per-Year rule. It just can't be done.

FYI, the IRS doesn't refer to direct transfers as rollovers, generally speaking - they call them trustee-to-trustee transfers. The "R" word is generally reserved for the indirect, 60-day type.

So - if you use an indirect rollover to move funds from one IRA to another, you now have limited yourself, with regard to those two IRAs. You cannot rollover money

from either IRA to any other IRA for 12 months - actually 365 days, 366 in leap years.

How about an example to 'splain this a little better?

Examples

Situation 1: Jane has 3 IRAs: IRA A, IRA B, and IRA C. There is $100,000 in each account. Jane wishes to move half of the money from IRA A into IRA B. If she takes a withdrawal from IRA A of $50,000 and receive a check for it, she can then deposit the check into IRA B within 60 days, and the rollover is complete.

At this point, Jane cannot rollover any of the remaining $50,000 in IRA A into IRA B or IRA C for 12 months. She furthermore cannot rollover any of the current $150,000 now residing in IRA B into IRA A or IRA C for 12 months. What Jane could do is rollover any amount she wishes from IRA C into either IRA A or IRA B - as long as IRA C hasn't been involved in an indirect rollover within 12 months.

Situation 2: Same situation as above, except Jane does a direct, trustee-to-trustee rollover of $50,000 from IRA A to IRA B. She is not limited at this point for making any other move with the funds in any of her IRAs. She could rollover the same $50,000 back into IRA A from IRA B using either method, but the indirect rollover would put her back into the limit mode described above. Jane is free to make any rollovers she wishes at this stage, since she used the trustee-to-trustee transfer.

Situation 3: Same facts as in Situation 1 above, except now Jane changes her mind about the rollover a week after she requested the check from IRA A, and she deposits it back into IRA A without ever depositing into IRA B. Regardless of the fact that Jane is now back where she started, this action is considered a rollover. This has now limited her ability to successfully rollover any amount from IRA A for a period of 12 months. The other IRAs are unaffected.

Situation 4: This one will be more complex, showing what might happen if you aren't paying attention. Same starting facts as the others. Jane does an indirect rollover of $50,000 from IRA A to IRA B on September 1. So far so good. But then, Jane decides she wants to rollover the remaining $50,000 from IRA A into IRA C, and she does this on December 1 of the same year. Then in January of the following year, Jane decides what she'd really like is to rollover all of the funds from IRA C into IRA A instead, so she takes the distribution of $150,000 from IRA C and deposit into IRA A account within 60 days.

What is going to happen? Well, if all of those things happened and none of the custodians stopped her, she'd have to pay tax on a distribution of $50,000 (plus any growth on that amount) from IRA A in the first year.

Since the rollover of $50,000 from IRA A to IRA C was within the 12 month period, this would be considered a disallowed rollover and therefore a taxable distribution. Since Jane pulled the money out before taxes were due, there is no additional consequence for her actions in the first year. If she had waited until after April 15 of the second year to withdraw the funds, she might have had to pay an additional 6% excess contribution tax on the

$50,000 disallowed rollover, since this would be considered a regular contribution to IRA C.

But part of the rollover from IRA C to IRA A, the amount less than the disallowed excess contribution and any associated growth, would be allowed as a completed rollover. Remember the prohibition is on rollovers **from** the involved accounts, and since IRA C had not been involved in a valid rollover within 12 months (since the rollover from IRA A had been disallowed), this amount is a valid rollover. Jane would still have to pull out the $50,000 (plus growth) from IRA A to avoid excess contribution tax.

In all of the situations above where the distribution became taxable, there could also be the 10% early distribution penalty applied unless one of the exceptions is met.

Admonition

So - what's the lesson here? Never, ever, ever do a 60-day rollover unless there is some mitigating circumstance requiring a 60-day rollover. And if you have to do the indirect 60-day rollover, make sure you mind your p's and q's with the accounts involved, so you don't get hung up on the one-rollover-per-year rule. Often, the IRA custodian will step in and explain the prohibition to you, but not always, and they're not responsible for your actions. If you do this and they let you get away with it, the entire tax bill is yours and yours alone.

20. Net Unrealized Appreciation (NUA)

This often-misunderstood section of the IRS code can be quite a benefit – if it happens to fit your situation. Net Unrealized Appreciation (NUA) refers to the increase in value of your company's stock held within your 401(k), either due to a company match or your own investment in the company stock within the 401(k). Other company-sponsored deferred accounts can apply here as well, but the primary type of account is the 401(k), so we'll refer to all company-sponsored tax-deferred accounts as 401(k)'s for the purpose of this discussion.

In order to take advantage of the NUA provision, first of all you must hold your company's stock in your 401(k), and you must be in a position to rollover the account. In other words, you must have separated from service, by leaving employment (voluntarily or involuntarily), or the 401(k) plan is being terminated.

As you consider the rollover of your funds, if the company stock has increased in value, you have unrealized appreciation, or rather appreciated value which has not yet been realized due to a sale of the stock. The IRS allows for this appreciation to be treated as a capital gain, which can result in much lower tax rates on the gain.

In order to take advantage of this treatment, the entire 401(k) account must be rolled over in one tax year, but there are a few things you must do differently from other rollovers: The company stock will be rolled over into a taxable (non-IRA) account, while everything else will be rolled over into a Traditional IRA or another company's plan.

When you roll over the company stock, this will be considered a distribution, and you will be required to pay the tax on the basis (or cost) of the stock as well as the 10% penalty if you're under age 55. Your employer or the plan custodian will have maintained records on your original cost of the stock.

As an example, let's say Dick has participated in his company's 401(k) plan for several years and he's ready to retire. Part of the 401(k) funds have been invested over the years in his company's stock, which has cost a total of $10,000 through the years. Dick's company has done well, and now his stock is worth $150,000 in the market. If Dick rolled over this stock into an IRA, he would eventually pay ordinary income tax on the growth of $140,000 – at whatever his current marginal income tax rate is (for example, let's use 25%). Instead of going that route, Dick decides to use the NUA provision in the tax law to his advantage.

So, Dick sets up a new IRA and a taxable account at the brokerage of his choice, and direct the 401(k) administrator to roll over his company stock to the taxable account, and all other funds to the IRA. When he rolls over the company stock into the taxable account, he will be taxed (at ordinary income tax rates plus the 10% penalty if he was under age 55) on the basis of the stock – which, from our example, was $10,000. Now, not only will the growth of the stock ($140,000) have a tax rate of 15% (or less) for capital gains, Dick also does not have to take required minimum distributions (RMD) from those funds.

He can leave the company stock in the taxable account for the rest of his life if he wishes, and hand it over to his heirs, who would receive a step-up in basis to the current value of the stock at Dick's passing.

Here's the math: Dick pays tax at our example rate of 25% on the $10,000 basis of the stock, or $2,500. Dick is over age 55, so no 10% penalty applies. Then, as he sells some of the stock, the total amount of capital gains tax would be 15% (at today's rates) of $140,000 (just the growth!) or $21,000. Compare that to the non-NUA treatment, where Dick would be taxed with ordinary income tax rates on the entire $150,000 stock value over time, for a total of $37,500! In this example, Dick saved a total of $14,000 in taxes! Wow…

Now, NUA treatment doesn't work for all situations. For example, if your company stock has only grown minimally in value, or has gone down in value, there is little or no benefit to utilizing the NUA option. Also, if the basis of the stock is fairly high relative to the growth, it might make sense to only apply NUA treatment to a portion of your company stock. And of course, NUA treatment is only available if you've left the company.

21. Things to Consider Before Rollover

Conventional wisdom has long told us that when we leave employment – either by taking another job, getting laid off, or retiring – it makes good sense to rollover our 401(k) plans to either an IRA or to our new employer's 401(k) plan if it makes sense.

However – and if you have read much of my writings, you know there's always a however in life – this decision isn't as cut-and-dried as conventional wisdom leads us to believe. As with just about every financial decision we make, it's not wise to go off willy-nilly without considering all of the benefits we're giving up. (and I don't cater much to the willy-nilly)

9 Special Considerations Before Rolling Over Your 401(k)

1. If you are happy with your former employer's plan, consider it well-managed, low cost, and possibly with some investment options not readily available (such as desirable mutual funds closed to new investors), you may want to leave the money in the plan intact. This would be especially beneficial if you don't have another employer plan to roll over into, or you are squeamish about establishing your own IRA.

2. Maintaining a 401(k) account could garner you some employer-sponsored financial advice. Some employers provide financial advice as an addtional benefit to

employees. Removal of your funds via a rollover would eliminate this benefit for you.

3. If you have commingled deductible and non-deducted IRA contributions in your IRA account, having an active 401(k) plan can help you to "separate" the deductible IRA assets from the non-deducted. See Chapter 58 for more about how this works. Essentially this benefit gives you a way to bypass the "little bit pregnant" rule wherein you must consider all IRA funds pro-rata when making distributions – a common issue when doing a Roth IRA conversion, for example. If you have no 401(k) plan, this option is lost.

4. If you have an investment in your former employer's stock in your 401(k), you need to consider the ramifications of utilizing the Net Unrealized Appreciation (NUA) option – before doing a rollover. Chapter 20 explains NUA, in case you need more details. The point is, if you've taken even a partial rollover of your 401(k) in a prior year, the NUA treatment or employer stock is no longer available to you.

5. If you think you may be returning to this employer, it might make sense to leave your funds where they are. This is especially true for government employers with section 457 plans – due to the nature of these plans' ability to provide you with retirement income without penalty much earlier than an IRA can. With the vagaries of governmental policy changes, if you've withdrawn and closed your account and come back to

work for the same agency, the old plan may no longer be available to you since you're a "new" participant.

6. If you're at or above age 55 and are not moving to a new employer (or are undertaking self-employment), maintaining the 401(k) plan gives you an option to begin taking distributions prior to age 59½ without penalty. If you move these funds over to an IRA, this option is lost.

7. On the off-chance you might need a loan from your retirement funds, you need to be aware that IRAs do not have this provision. Retain at least some balance in the 401(k) plan if you might need this option – but also you should check with your plan administrator to see if this option is available for non-employee plan participants, because it might not be (and actually, it likely is not). But keeping in mind #5 above, if you've maintained a healthy balance in the plan and you return to work with this same employer, you'd have a much larger account to work with if you needed to borrow.

8. Funds in a 401(k) account are protected by ERISA – and as such are generally not available to creditors. Depending upon the state you live in, IRA assets may be available to your creditors in the event of a bankruptcy. If you'd like to bone up more on this, see Chapter 10. At any rate, ERISA protection is pretty much an absolute, so this is yet another reason you might consider leaving funds in a former employer's 401(k) plan.

9. Take your after-tax contributions out first, if your plan happens to include these. If you've made after-tax contributions, as some plans allow, it makes sense to

separate these contributions from the pre-taxed amounts. You can convert these contributions directly over to a Roth IRA in most cases. This is because the 401(k) isn't subject to the "little bit pregnant" rule alluded to earlier. Once you've removed the after-tax contributions and put them into a Roth IRA, you can then rollover the rest of your 401(k) to an IRA if it makes sense.

I don't claim this to be an exhaustive list of all the reasons you need to stop and think about it before rolling over a 401(k) plan, but we've hit the high points.

22. Taxes and Rollovers

Taking early withdrawals from your retirement plans is rarely a good idea, and should only be considered when it's the last possible option available to you, generally speaking. But this article is more about the pain you could experience if you don't handle a rollover correctly – bypassing the trustee-to-trustee transfer option and going with an indirect rollover.

Withholding Rule For Indirect Rollovers

In general, if you take an early withdrawal (pre-age 59½) from an IRA or a Qualified Retirement Plan (QRP) that includes pre-tax money, the custodian of the account is required to withhold and pay to the IRS 20% of the pre-tax amount withdrawn. This can still be a tax-free transaction if you finish the indirect rollover process correctly and place the entire amount of the distribution back into an IRA or QRP within 60 days. However, if you don't complete the indirect rollover within the allotted time, you're likely to get a tax surprise.

A transaction like this is called an "indirect rollover", as opposed to a direct or a trustee-to-trustee rollover. In order to complete the indirect rollover within 60 days, you will need to come up with the 20% that was withheld in order to have a full rollover – otherwise you'll have to pay tax and a penalty on the amount that was not rolled over (the withheld amount).

An Example

For example, let's say Jane is 50 years of age, and she has a 401(k) from a former employer that she'd like to rollover into her IRA account. The 401(k) has a total of $50,000 in it. For whatever reason, Jane opted to have the 401(k) custodian send her a check for the amount, which she then plans on sending to the IRA custodian for deposit (within the allowable 60 day period, as an indirect rollover).

A 401(k) custodian is required to withhold 20% from any distribution that is not a rollover. Lo and behold, when the check arrives, it's only made out for $40,000! This is because the custodian was required to withhold 20%. So now, since Jane doesn't have any savings to speak of, she can only send the $40,000 over to the IRA custodian. Guess what? Come tax time, Jane will have to include the "lost" $10,000 as income, plus she'll get to pay a 10% early withdrawal penalty as well. So if Jane is in the 25% tax bracket, she gets to pay $3,500 in tax and penalties (25% times $10,000 plus 10% times $10,000).

Now, the original 401(k) worth $50,000 has been reduced to an IRA worth $40,000 and a tax refund of $6,500 (since $10,000 was withheld and her tax and penalties were $3,500). This swift little maneuver has cost Jane 7% of her retirement plan! Plus, she has lost tax-deferral on $10,000.

ALWAYS Do the Direct Rollover

For this reason, whenever possible, you always should do a direct, or trustee-to-trustee transfer when rolling over IRA and QRP funds to a new account. When you do a trustee-to-trustee rollover, no withholding applies, so you don't have to make up any difference, and your tax-deferred amount remains intact.

It's important to note that in our example above, if Jane had had the $10,000 available in savings or elsewhere to make up the difference for the withholding, she could still complete the indirect rollover without tax or penalty by sending a total of $50,000 to the IRA custodian within 60 days. Then when she files her taxes for the year, the $10,000 withheld would become either a refund or a reduction in the amount of tax Jane had to pay for the year.

23. Waivers for the 60-Day Rollover

There are all sorts of problems that can crop up when attempting to complete a 60-day rollover of qualified funds to an IRA. Sometimes you can be granted an automatic waiver of the 60-day rule, but only if ALL of the following apply:

- The financial institution receives the funds on your behalf before the end of the 60-day rollover period.

- You followed all the procedures set by the financial institution for depositing the funds into an eligible retirement plan within the 60-day period (including giving instructions to deposit the funds into an eligible retirement plan).

- The funds are not deposited into an eligible retirement plan within the 60-day rollover period solely because of an error on the part of the financial institution.

- The funds are deposited into an eligible retirement plan within 1 year from the beginning of the 60-day rollover period.

- It would have been a valid rollover if the financial institution had deposited the funds as instructed.

If the above conditions do not apply, you can still request a ruling from the IRS, called a Private Letter Ruling (PLR); if you still think your circumstances merit the inclusion of your rollover even though it was beyond the 60-day period.

When making a determination on your request, the IRS will consider all of the following details:

- Whether errors were made by the financial institution (other than those described under "Automatic waiver", earlier);

- Whether you were unable to complete the rollover due to death, disability, hospitalization, incarceration, restrictions imposed by a foreign country or postal error;

- Whether you used the amount distributed (for example, in the case of payment by check, whether you cashed the check); and

- How much time has passed since the date of distribution?

If you are planning to request a PLR, keep in mind the costs can be quite high. In addition to the $3,000 user fee to the IRS, the cost for a tax attorney to prepare the request can be anywhere from $3,000 to $10,000 or more, depending upon the complexity. And there's no guarantee that you will receive a positive ruling.

Once again, the problems you find with the 60-day rollover highlight the benefit of doing the relatively painless trustee-to-trustee transfer.

Roth Conversions

24. Intro to Roth Conversion

There is a provision in the tax law that allows an individual to convert funds to a Roth (the IRA, not David Lee) from a Traditional IRA or a qualified, tax-deferred plan like a 401(k). This means you are taking a distribution from the IRA or qualified plan and moving the money to a Roth IRA account. The amount distributed from the non-Roth account will be subject to tax but not penalties, as long as you complete the conversion.

This provides a way for you to place monies into a Roth IRA much more quickly than making regular annual contributions to the account. This maneuver has been available for quite some time now, and as of tax year 2010, conversions are available to folks of all income levels.

There are several things to consider before you do a Roth Conversion.

Factors to Consider Before Converting to a Roth IRA

- If you convert funds from an IRA to a Roth IRA, it is most advantageous if you are able to pay the tax on the conversion from funds outside of your IRAs. If you can't do this, realize any funds used to pay tax on the conversion will also be subject to the 10% early withdrawal penalty if no other exception applies and you're under age 59½.

- What is your outlook on tax rates? A Roth conversion, especially when there is a sizeable amount to convert, may be taxed at some very high rates, depending upon your situation. For example, a couple who would normally have a MAGI of $110,000 would have a marginal 25% rate. Add in a $200,000 Roth IRA conversion, and a portion of those funds would be taxed at as high as the 33% rate. It only makes sense to convert if you believe the rates in the future would be higher than the rate you'd pay tax on the conversion today.

- Does your IRA contain nondeductible contributions? If, in years past, you have contributed nondeductible amounts to your IRA due to income limits, the Roth conversion of those amounts is a no-brainer for you. However, you must be careful about how you do a conversion in this case, because any funds other than your nondeductible contributions would be considered taxable upon the conversion. *(see Note a bit later for additional explanation)*

- When do you plan to access your funds? If it's going to be several years (10 or more) then you will have a better chance of having recouped the tax outlay by way of the tax-free growth in the account.

If you need to access the funds from this account much sooner, bear in mind funds converted to a Roth IRA can't be distributed without penalty until five years after the conversion. This could throw a wrench in the entire process if you needed access sooner.

Roth Conversions

If you don't plan to ever access these funds, a conversion may make sense for you, since a Roth IRA has no Required Minimum Distribution (RMD). *Funds converted to a Roth IRA cannot be withdrawn without penalty until five years after the conversion.* This way, you won't have to deplete your IRA balance (after age 70½), and your heirs will reap the benefits of a much larger account, all tax free, with tax deferral continuing throughout your heirs' lifetimes. They will have to take RMDs from the account, though.

Note: *A complication comes up when you have a combination of non-deductible contributions and otherwise taxable growth and/or deductible contributions housed in the same account: IRA rules require that distributions (including conversions) must be taken out ratably, or in the proportions of the entire account. See Chapter 58 for more on the pro rata distribution rules.*

For example, if Jane had an IRA with a $100,000 balance, of which $50,000 is non-deductible contributions, $30,000 is deductible contributions, and $20,000 is growth, then for every dollar Jane converts to a Roth IRA, fifty cents would be taxed and fifty cents would be tax-free return of basis.

One way around this is to rollover the amounts above and beyond Jane's nondeductible contributions into a 401(k) or other eligible plan (but not an IRA), and then convert the remaining amount (the nondeductible contributions) to her Roth IRA. This would effectively be a tax-free maneuver. **Consult your tax advisor to make sure you're doing this correctly.**

25. 5-year Rules

In case the rules surrounding Roth IRAs weren't confusing enough so far, there are actually TWO different 5-year rules that can apply to your Roth IRA account.

5-Year Rule #1: The Account's Age

In general, the first 5-year period begins on January 1 of the tax year when you established and first funded the account. This 5-year rule is important in determining if any distributions you receive from the account are qualified. In order to be qualified, a withdrawal must occur at least 5 years after the account establishment date (January 1 of the year you first funded the account). In addition to the 5-year rule, one of the following conditions must also apply in order for your distribution to be considered qualified:

- You are over age 59½

- You are disabled

- You (the account owner) are deceased

- The distribution is for a qualified first home purchase

See the IRS' flowchart below in order to determine if your distribution is qualified.

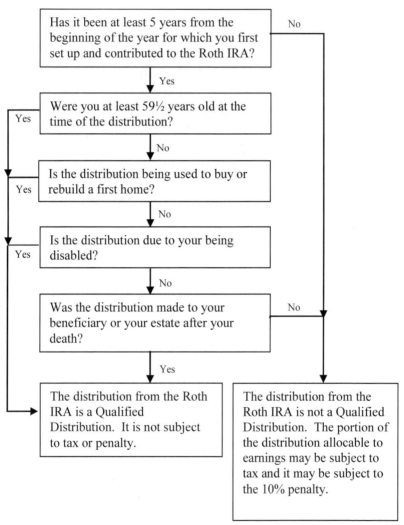

Source: IRS Publication 590

5-Year Rule #2: Age of a Conversion

This 5-year period begins on January 1 of the year of a conversion to a Roth IRA from a Traditional IRA or from a qualified retirement plan such as a 401(k). If, within 5 years of the conversion, you withdraw *any of the money that was taxed during the conversion*, an additional 10% penalty tax will be applied to the withdrawal. The penalty also applies to post-conversion earnings on the amounts converted within the previous 5 years. Possible exceptions to this rule are as follows:

- You have reached age 59½

- You are disabled

- You are the beneficiary of a deceased IRA owner

- You use the distribution to pay certain qualified first-time homebuyer amounts

- The distributions are part of a series of substantially equal payments

- You have significant unreimbursed medical expenses

- You are paying medical insurance premiums after losing your job

- The distributions are not more than your qualified higher education expenses

- The distribution is due to an IRS levy of the qualified plan

- The distribution is a qualified reservist distribution

- The distribution is a qualified disaster recovery assistance distribution

- The distribution is a qualified recovery assistance distribution

Why These Rules Are Important: Distribution Ordering Rules

These two five-year rules above come into play when considering the order in which distributions are attributed. The IRS has specific rules determining just which money is coming out of your account and how it is to be treated, depending on if it's qualified or not. The order of distribution is as follows:

- Regular contributions

- Conversion and rollover contributions, on a first-in, first-out basis, meaning the total of conversions and rollovers from the earliest year come out first. These conversions and rollovers are further sorted as follows:

    o Taxable portion (the portion taxed during the conversion or rollover)

    o Non-taxable portion

    o Earnings on all contributions

It should be noted, in determining the amounts for conversion and rollover contributions, certain aggregation rules apply:

- Add all distributions from all your Roth IRAs during the year together.

- Add all regular contributions made for the year (including contributions made after the close of the year, but before the due date of your return) together. Add this total to the total undistributed regular contributions made in prior years.

- Add all conversion and rollover contributions made during the year together. For purposes of the ordering rules, in the case of any conversion or rollover in which the conversion or rollover distribution is made in 2011 and the conversion or rollover contribution is made in 2012, treat the conversion or rollover contribution as contributed before any other conversion or rollover contributions made in 2012.

Of course, the regular contributions can always be taken out of the account tax free (no 5-year rule applies). Above and beyond the contributions, your two 5-year rules kick in on the rest of the types of funds in your account.

If your Roth account was established:	And you are:	Type of funds available without penalty:
Any time	Less than 59½	Contributions only
Less than five years ago	At least 59½	Contributions only
More than five years ago, less than five years since conversion	Less than 59½	Contributions only
	At least 59½	Contributions and growth attributed to contributions
More than five years ago, more than five years since conversion	Less than 59½	Contributions and converted amounts
	At least 59½	All funds in the account

Source: IRS

26. Conversion Strategy: Fill out the bracket

One strategy to consider as you think about making Roth IRA conversions is the idea of "filling out the bracket". With this strategy, you figure out your income level and what income tax bracket you're in, and if it makes sense, convert enough of your IRA or QRP to effectively use up the remainder of your tax bracket.

Of course, this mostly makes sense in the lower tax brackets, but for some folks with potentially high future income it may be appropriate at higher tax brackets. Your feeling on this also depends on what you think will happen with tax rates as you get to the point where you're ready to retire – and if you're like me, you've got to believe tax rates are on the rise.

The following table illustrates the highest income you could have within each tax bracket, using the rates for a single taxpayer and a married taxpayer, using only the Standard Deduction for 2012, with one exemption for the single taxpayer and two for the married taxpayer. Add $3,800 (for 2012) to the figure for each additional exemption claimed, and add the difference of your itemized deductions above the standard.

Maximum Income in Each Bracket w/Standard Deduction Only – 2012		
Tax Bracket	**Single, 1 Exemption**	**Married, 2 Exemptions**
0%	$9,750	$19,500
10%	$18,450	$36,900
15%	$45,100	$90,200
25%	$95,400	$162,200
28%	$188,400	$236,950
33%	$398,100	$407,850
35%	Over $398,100	Over $407,850

Source: IRS

To use the above table, calculate your income – from wages, salaries, tips, dividends, interest, short-term capital gains, rental income, etc. Figure out which tax bracket you fit into, based on the table (the table takes your exemption and standard deductions into account, so don't subtract those). Subtract your income amount from the amount for your applicable bracket: the remainder is how much you could convert to a Roth IRA while remaining in the same tax bracket.

As an example, let's say Dick is single with no dependents. Dick's total income for the year will be $30,000. When we go to the table we see Dick is in the 15% bracket, and he could convert up to $15,100 to a Roth IRA without bumping himself up above the 15% bracket. The additional tax on the conversion amount would be $2,265.

For another example, let's say Dick and Jane are married, and their household income is also $30,000. According to the table, Dick and Jane are in the 10% bracket, and they could convert as much as $6,900 without going above the 10% bracket. Plus if Dick and Jane have two kids who are dependents, the additional exemptions would increase the number by an additional $7,600 ($3,800 per dependent exemption) to a total of $14,500 of "headroom" in the tax bracket.

Now, you might be saying to yourself, that's all well and good, but how many families of four have the wherewithal to undertake a Roth conversion in those circumstances? After all, that would be an additional tax of $1,450! You're right, it may not be terribly practical for folks in those particular circumstances – but consider someone who is semi-retired, who has very little taxable earned income beyond some interest and dividends. How about a married, retired individual, with part-time work earnings of $10,000? This individual could convert as much as $9,500 to a Roth IRA – *and owe no income tax at all!*

As I've mentioned before, unless you're very, very competent with preparing your own income taxes, please, do yourself a favor and run any plans of this nature past a tax professional. It can be well worth the cost – you don't want to make mistakes on this sort of thing! And if you rely on a box as your tax advisor, don't expect the box to represent your interests before the IRS.

97

27. Conversion Strategy: Remember Social Security

Social Security benefit taxation often gets short shrift while considering a Roth IRA Conversion. In addition, your Medicare Part B premium is subject to adjustment (and not in the good direction) with an increase to your overall income from a Roth Conversion.

Understandably, this hasn't really hit the radar for most conversion topics, because this is primarily important to folks at lower incomes. So if you're one of those fatcats with an annual retirement income projected above $100,000, then you might not want to bother reading any further – this chapter likely doesn't apply to you. *(But look at the note at the end of the chapter before you leave!)*

However, (and there's always a however in life), this will be important to consider if you are in a position to reduce your provisional income (your net non-Social Security income plus ½ of your Social Security benefit) to a level below $44,000 – even more so if you can reduce it to below $32,000. Those are the numbers for Married Filing Jointly – the figures for Single, Qualifying Widow(er), Head of Household, or Married Filing Separately are $34,000 and $25,000, respectively. And these numbers have not been subject to indexation (adjustment due to inflation) as long as they've been in existence.

Now, it may seem like this is a pretty insurmountable position to be in: after all, you need an income of (for example) $60,000 in order to just get by! Imagine, though, what would happen if you were able to take a large portion of your required $60,000 from a tax-free source, such as a Roth IRA. In some cases, you might be able to get by without having to pay tax on any or a large portion of your Social Security benefits.

The Facts

I guess I got a little ahead of myself – let's back up and look at the facts. If your net Adjusted Gross Income (AGI, not including line 20b from Form 1040) plus ½ of your Social Security benefit is less than $32,000 ($25,000 for Singles, et al), then none of your Social Security benefit is taxed. If the amount described above is greater than $32,000 but not more than $44,000 (between $25,000 and $34,000 for Singles), then 50% of your Social Security benefit will be taxed. If the calculation is above $44,000 ($34,000 for Singles), then 85% of your Social Security benefit will be taxed.

Example (*uses 2012 tax tables – your mileage may vary)

Let's say for example John and Mary's lifestyle requires an income of $60,000, and they have a combined Social Security benefit of $25,000. So, John and Mary take a total of $35,000 from their IRAs (total balance of $500,000) to make up the difference. Running the calculation, when we add ½ of the SS benefit to the rest of the income ($12,500 plus $35,000) we get $47,500. Since this is greater than $44,000, 85% of the SS benefits are taxed.

If John and Mary decided to convert 20% of their IRAs to Roth IRAs ($100,000), now instead of taking $35,000 from the Traditional IRA each year, they could take $28,000 from the Traditional IRA and $7,000 from the Roth. Re-running the calculation, now ½ of SS benefit plus AGI ($12,500 plus $28,000) equals $40,500. After the Roth conversion, only 50% of the SS benefit is taxed! Granted, in the year of the Roth conversion, John and Mary had to pay considerably more tax on the conversion amount, an additional $23,962, but this pays off in reduced taxable Social Security (SS) benefit after just over 10 years.

Taking this a step further, if John and Mary decided to convert 40% of their IRAs to Roth IRAs ($200,000), they can eliminate taxation of SS benefits altogether. Now they can reduce the amount they withdraw from the Traditional IRA to only $21,000, and withdraw $14,000 (tax free) from the Roth. Running the calculation again, we come up with $33,500 ($12,500 plus $21,000) – we're at less than the $34,000 limit. At this level, NONE of the Social Security benefit is taxed. Again, there is a significant tax cost in the year of conversion ($53,902), which is paid off in reduced taxes in just over 10 years at today's rates. With both examples, if when future tax rates increase, the payoff is even faster.

So you can see how this could be a great strategy for folks who are capable of reducing their income component by such a factor. There's also the added benefit of reduced amounts against which Required Minimum Distributions are calculated. As you reach the RMD age limit (70½), you may have determined you don't need the amount required as income. If you can reduce the Traditional IRA balance by converting a good portion to a Roth IRA, the RMD amount will be less by proportion.

Of course, you could also reduce the tax hit by drawing out the time within which you do the conversions – such as splitting up the $200,000 over four years, for example – this way you'd have much more of the conversion taxed at lower rates. Obviously, your situation is going to vary from the example, so work closely with your tax advisor as you make plans.

Note: Keep in mind this strategy could work for literally anyone at any income level – as long as the income isn't from a fixed source, such as a Traditional pension. If it's from investment accounts, IRAs, annuities, or some qualified retirement plan, then you should consider this strategy to see if it makes sense for you.

28. Structuring Your Conversion

Earlier in this book I briefly covered the topic of Recharacterization. The example I gave was pretty simplistic – you converted an amount, and decided later to recharacterize the funds back to an IRA. What if it gets complicateder?

There are some steps you can take in your conversion that which will help you to recharacterize later, if the occasion should arise. These steps to structure the conversion are by no means required, they'd fit into a "simplifying your life" category, more than anything – or what I have heard referred to as a CYA* activity.

Structuring a Conversion

If you think you'll want to come back and consider recharacterizing some of your conversion, you should start off with a brand-new Roth IRA account as the receiver of the conversion. This way you don't have to worry about separating the money later on during a recharacterization.

In addition, depending upon the volatility of your holdings, you might want to chunk things up even further – especially if we're dealing with a sizeable amount of money. You might consider chunking your account into separate IRAs for large-caps, small-caps, and global stocks, at the very least. There's no limit to the number of IRA accounts you could split the holdings into, so if you wanted, you could open a new Roth account for each asset class you own.

The point to all of this splitting is, in the event one of the assets dramatically reduces in value through the year, since you've kept them segregated it will be simple to recharacterize just one asset. This way you can keep from paying higher tax on a dramatically reduced asset.

The IRS doesn't always treat all IRAs as a single entity.   But wait! Doesn't the IRS treat all IRAs as one account? Hold on there: You're making the assumption that there is consistency in the rules – and consistency in the rules would be a huge departure from the IRS' proud track record. Besides, if the rules were consistent and made sense, then what would guys like me write about?

In the case of recharacterizing funds converted to a Roth IRA, the IRS only considers the account you converted into. This is why it's important to (at the very least) start with a fresh new account – because any recharacterization in an account commingled with prior conversions and/or contributions will likely dilute the effect of the recharacterization. At the very least, commingling conversion funds will really complicate things, and lead to some potentially uncomfortable moments during an audit.

The more you've chunked your account, the easier it will be to choose only those funds which have fallen in value to recharacterize. Otherwise the benefit is diluted by any increases on other holdings.

* *CYA in this sense stands for "Chunk Your Accounts". You may have a different interpretation.*

29. Three Tax-Free Conversions

So you're wondering if there is a way to do this Roth Conversion thing tax free? There are actually several, three of which I'll list here. These may match your circumstance or perhaps spur an idea.

After-Tax IRA Contributions

If your IRA is composed only of after-tax (non-deducted) contributions, you can convert those funds over to a Roth IRA without tax consequence. This is because the funds were taxed before you contributed them to the IRA, and so no tax is due when you convert the funds to a Roth IRA.

The "gotcha" in this is the IRA must include ONLY non-deducted, after-tax contributions. Plus this must be the only IRA you own – see Chapter 58 for the "Turns Out You CAN Be A Little Bit Pregnant" rule. There's also a way around the "Pregnant" rule described there.

With this method in mind, you may have thought of a strategy for getting money into your Roth IRA account if your income is too high for regular contributions into the Roth account. You could make a non-deductible contribution to a Traditional IRA, and then some time afterward (it probably is best to allow some time to pass, so the overall activity isn't considered a single event) convert the Traditional IRA to a Roth IRA account. This is a strategy many folks have used for some time now, and it appears that the IRS doesn't have any issues with it. The

105

trick to ensuring this process remains legal is to do the steps as separate activities – even though your plan is to eventually have the money in a Roth IRA, the first thing you're doing is making a non-deductible contribution to a Traditional IRA. Allow time to pass, and then move on with the conversion.

After-Tax Qualified Retirement Plan Contributions

If you happen to have after-tax contributions to a Qualified Retirement Plan (QRP) such as a 401(k), these can be rolled over tax free if you've terminated employment – without having to worry about the "Pregnant" rule I mentioned above. This is because QRP funds are treated differently, and as such you are allowed to move specific contribution money separate from other contribution money (e.g., pre-tax contributions separate from after-tax contributions).

This can be a very good way to bump up your Roth IRA holdings without incurring additional tax.

Zero Tax Bracket

If you have no or very low taxable income, in other words, if you're below the 10% tax bracket, any funds you distribute from your IRA up to the limit – which would be your Adjusted Gross Income (AGI) minus your exemptions and itemized or standard deductions and any tax credits – would be tax free. (See the table in Chapter 26 for the brackets for 2012.) Granted, this is likely to be a somewhat small amount for most people in this situation, but for others, such as business owners or farmers with carried-over Net Operating Losses, it could be sizeable. See Chapter 33 for more information on NOL carryovers and Roth IRA conversions.

An IRA Owner's Manual

30. Three Things to Consider

There are a lot of reasons why a Roth IRA Conversion might not be the best idea for a lot of folks. Here are three really good reasons why you probably should reconsider.

Three Reasons You May Not Want to Convert to a Roth IRA

"Same as it ever was..." Several factors must be considered when determining if a Roth conversion makes sense for you:

1. the amount of the conversion

2. your conversion tax rate

3. your earnings on the converted account

4. the amount you withdraw from the Roth account

5. the date you begin withdrawing the funds from the Roth account

If you would have begun taking the withdrawals on the same date (#5) regardless of the account (Traditional or Roth), in the same net (after tax) amount (#4), at the same tax rate (#2) – assuming your earnings would be the same either way – there is no advantage to the Roth conversion.

In order for there to be a benefit to the conversion, one or more of the following must happen:

- the date you begin taking distributions must be later (taking advantage of the fact that there's no RMD);

- the amount you would take as a distribution must be less (since there's no tax); and/or

- the tax you pay on the distribution would have been higher than the conversion rate.

If future taxes are lower or the converted funds fall drastically in value, a Roth conversion may be a bad move after all.

A downward spiral. If the value of the investments in the account actually reduce in value, you'll be in a worse position if you convert to a Roth IRA. For example, if your IRA was worth $100,000 when you converted it, if your tax rate was 25% then the tax cost of the conversion is $25,000. If the value of the account subsequently fell to $50,000 (of course, some time after the time limit has expired for recharacterization) — now the overall rate the conversion cost you has inflated to 50%.

An unlikely downward spiral. By the same token, if (heaven forbid) the tax rates are lower in the future, it wouldn't make any sense for you to do a Roth conversion. The more likely event is your personal tax rate might be a lot less — especially possible if in retirement you have a pretty low-cost lifestyle.

If you converted funds and the applicable rate was 25% and then later on in your life your income needs had you down in one of the lower brackets, you probably over-paid for the privilege of doing the conversion.

The game changes. What happens to you if Congress decides this Roth deal is just too good? Maybe they'll start requiring distributions of the original account owner – or restrict the amount of time your heirs can stretch payments? It's really impossible to guess what Congress might do – but given the potential cost of lost tax revenues from Roth accounts, it's not hard to believe the rules could be changed to have a negative impact on your converted account.

Of course, this is not an exhaustive list – just a few good reasons why you really need to think this over before you do a Roth conversion. Don't let the hype over the idea of doing a Roth Conversion let you get caught in a wave.

An IRA Owner's Manual

31. Direct Conversion from 401(k)

Back in the olden days prior to 2008, it was against the rules to convert funds directly from a 401(k) plan (or other CODA plan, like a 403(b) or 457) to a Roth IRA. At the time, you were required to do the "conversion two-step" wherein you would first rollover or direct-transfer your funds from the 401(k) plan to a Traditional IRA, then do a conversion from the Trad IRA into your Roth IRA. This was an unnecessarily complicated process, and the IRS logically ~~waited until it got ridiculous and then relented~~ listened to the concerns of taxpayers, allowing a direct conversion from these qualified retirement accounts into a Roth IRA.

The process is identical to the process for converting from a Traditional IRA to a Roth IRA. You can make this conversion from your or your spouse's:

- Employer's qualified pension, profit-sharing or stock bonus plan (including a 401(k) plan);

- Annuity plan;

- Tax-sheltered annuity plan (section 403(b) plan); or

- Governmental deferred compensation plan (section 457 plan).

You are allowed to convert all or part of the account. Any pre-tax amount converted must be reported as income in the year of the conversion.

The conversion can be done either via a direct trustee-to-trustee transfer or a rollover. In general, the trustee-to-trustee transfer is the preferred method since a rollover involves making a check payable to you, which requires the payor to withhold 20% of the distribution. Any amount not successfully converted within 60 days would be taxable AND subject to the 10% penalty unless other conditions applied.

So in other words, when you convert these funds over to your Roth account, in order to pay the tax on the withdrawal you'll need to either hold out a portion and pay the 10% penalty on those funds, or pay the tax from another source.

32. Conversions and the Inherited Plan

If you have an IRA or a 401(k) you've inherited, you may wonder if it is possible to convert the account over into a Roth IRA. After all, you've got to take RMD (Required Minimum Distributions) from the account since it's inherited, why couldn't you just pay all the tax upfront and roll it over?

Well, there are two answers to this question, one for inherited IRAs, and one for inherited qualified retirement plans (QRPs, such as 401(k) or 403(b) plans). And like many other things in this wonderful tax code of ours – the two kinds of plans are treated differently *today*, but may be subject to change in the future.

It should be noted that we're talking about *non-spouse beneficiaries* here. A spouse has pretty much the same rights as the decedent (original, now deceased, owner) had, so if the decedent was eligible for a Roth conversion, the spouse most likely is as well.

Inherited IRA

For an inherited IRA, current law does not allow you to convert the funds to a Roth IRA. This is pretty much cut-and-dried, with no interpretation necessary.

There is a great deal of conjecture about whether or not Congress will specifically change this ruling to match the QRP rule – since the QRP rule has only been available for a year or so. Until it's actually undertaken, this rule will continue to apply.

Inherited QRP

If you've inherited a qualified retirement plan (QRP), this account IS eligible for conversion to a Roth IRA. The new Roth IRA (and it must be a new account) must be titled as inherited, just the same as if you were rolling over the QRP funds into a Traditional IRA. The new Roth IRA would continue to be subject to RMD, however tax would have been paid up front so future RMD would be tax-free.

In the year of the conversion, you would still have to take your regular taxable RMD from the QRP, but the remainder of the account would be eligible for the Roth conversion. Keep in mind, this conversion has to be a direct (trustee-to-trustee) conversion into the Roth IRA.

33. Conversion Planning for the Small Business Owner

Continuing with the discussion about Roth IRA conversions –there is an opportunity for the small business owner or farmer which may be quite useful. Many small business owners and farmers have large Net Operating Loss (NOL) carryovers from previous tax years, since NOL can only be deducted to the extent of the individuals' Adjusted Gross Income. Excess NOL can be carried over for up to 20 years.

For the small business owner or farmer who has retired and closed his business, a large NOL can be difficult to utilize – especially if his income is small in relation to the NOL. If the small business owner or farmer has an IRA, there is a unique opportunity to convert a portion of his IRA to a Roth IRA equal to the carried over NOL, thereby converting the funds to a tax-free account with no tax owed.

The reason this is important is because carried over NOL disappears when the taxpayer dies. If the NOL is large enough that normal income (or Required Minimum Distributions) doesn't utilize the NOL completely, then this opportunity can help to create tax-free income for the taxpayer in the future.

This method is put into action by determining the amount of the NOL for the taxpayer, either carried over or generated in the current year. You can determine this amount from your prior years' tax returns and business records. Once you've discovered the amount of NOL available, a corresponding amount could be converted from your Traditional IRA to a Roth IRA. The NOL would be applied to the conversion income, making the conversion tax-free.

Note: estates and trusts can also have NOL, but this provision is not pertinent to estates and trusts.

34. SGLI Payout Conversion

Introduction

On May 20, 2008, Congress passed H.R. 6081, the Heroes Earnings Assistance and Relief Tax Act (also known as the HEART Act or Heroes Act), which was signed into law on June 17, 2008. One of the major provisions related to retirement accounts (IRAs and qualified accounts) is the ability to rollover SGLI (Servicemember's Group Life Insurance) payments to a Roth IRA or a Coverdell ESA.

Contributions of military death gratuities to Roth IRAs and Coverdell ESAs

The Act permits an individual who receives a military death gratuity or Servicemembers' Group Life Insurance ("SGLI") program payment to contribute the funds to a Roth IRA, or to one or more Coverdell education savings accounts.

Such contributions will be treated as rollover contributions to the Roth IRA or Coverdell ESA accounts, not subject to normal income or contribution limits. The maximum amount an individual can contribute to a Roth IRA and/or one or more Coverdell education savings accounts under this provision is limited to the sum of the gratuity and SGLI payments the individual receives.

In the event of a subsequent non-qualified distribution from the Roth IRA or the Coverdell education savings account, the amount of the distribution attributable to the contribution of the military death gratuity or SGLI payment is treated as nontaxable investment in the contract. This provision is generally effective with respect to payments made on account of deaths from injuries occurring on or after June 17, 2008.

This could make a profound difference for your taxes in the future.

For SGLI or military death gratuity payments due to a death occurring after June 17, 2008, you have one year from the date the payment is received to make the rollover. As always, if you have questions, talk to your financial advisor – she should be able to help you out with this.

35. Recharacterization

"Drizzle, Drazzle, Drozzle, Drome – time for zis one to come home." – Mr. Wizard

So you've done a Roth Conversion and now you're ready to do your taxes and (horrors!) you see the bill for the conversion: Yikes! Somehow a simple decimal point miscalculation has caused your nice little conversion to run up a HUGE tax bill. What to do?

Well, just the same as with Tooter the Turtle in the old cartoon, you can follow Mr. Wizard's advice and "be just what youse is, not what youse is not". In other words, you can undo the conversion, so you are back where you started. This is called a Recharacterization of the IRA.

The Great Undo

When you get yourself into such a situation, a complete "undo" is the cleanest way to go about this. So what you do is simply move the holdings back into the IRA account from the Roth, and file Form 8606 with your tax return. The recharacterization must be complete by the deadline for filing your return plus extensions, which means by October 15 of the following year for most folks.

On Form 8606, you'll indicate the amount converted to the Roth IRA, then indicate how much was recharacterized, and show the gain or loss on the funds, as well. This is one reason why it makes very good sense to open a new Roth account for each year's conversion. Once the deadline for recharacterization has passed, you

121

can rollover the converted funds into your regular Roth account to reduce paperwork (but of course, you don't have to do this).

One additional reason many folks decide to recharacterize their Roth conversion is because the value of their holdings in the account has decreased, and they don't want to pay tax on the higher value.

For example, if Dick converted $10,000 to a Roth account and the market took a 40% dive (like that's never happened, right?) – when it comes time to pay taxes, Dick would owe (for example) 25% on the originally-converted $10,000, while his account is only worth $6,000 now. For Dick, it's just too much to stomach, so he decides to recharacterize. After 30 days, Dick can then convert the funds again at the new, lower value, and forestall the tax until the following tax year, since presumably this is the following year from the original conversion by now. Otherwise Dick would need to delay re-conversion until the following tax year (and at least 30 days after the recharacterization).

Inherited IRAs

36. Splitting an Inherited IRA

These things can give you a splitting headache.

In the case of an IRA, often it is desirable to split an account into two (or more) accounts in order to better accommodate a distribution plan which would play out upon the death of the primary owner of the account. This can be done prior to the death of the IRA owner, or it could be done after the death of the IRA owner, as long as it's accomplished before the end of the year following the year of death.

Why is this important?

When an IRA is inherited by a non-spouse individual, the individual is required to begin taking distributions from the IRA, based either upon the heir's own age or the age of the decedent. In most cases when the beneficiary is younger than the decedent, it is advantageous to stretch those payments out over the longer period of time.

If there is more than one beneficiary, unless the IRA is split, the Required Minimum Distributions will be based upon the attained age of the "designated beneficiary" – who is by default the oldest beneficiary of the group as of September 30 of the year following the year of death.

If you've split the IRA into separate IRAs for each beneficiary, each titled as "John Jones, deceased, FBO Jane Brown" (probably not exactly like that, because the names will be different in almost all cases), then the individual IRAs can be distributed according to the age of the individual beneficiary. <u>The IRA must be split by December 31 of the year following the year of death.</u>

Note: bear in mind you don't have to have the IRA split into separate IRAs for each beneficiary by September 30 of the year following the year of death – this is just the administrative date for determination of the designated beneficiary. In the event the IRA is split into separate inherited IRAs by December 31 of the year following the year of death, then administratively the designated beneficiary of each separate IRA as of September 30 would be the individual FBO owner of the account.

37. Distribution Period When a Beneficiary is Not Named

We've talked about all kinds of issues surrounding distribution periods, but there's at least one more facet of distribution periods we have not addressed just yet. What happens when there is no designated beneficiary for the IRA account? More specifically, what is the longest distribution period heirs are allowed to stretch an IRA when there is no designated beneficiary?

As with most questions put forth to the IRS, there's more than one answer. So, here are the answers: **5** or **15.3**. If you're the bottom-line type, you can quit reading now.

Oh, right, you need more details: The answer is 5 years if the IRA owner died *prior to* his Required Beginning Date (RBD), which is April 1 of the year following the year in which he reaches age 70½, regardless of whether or not a distribution has already been taken. The answer is 15.3 years if the IRA owner died on or after his RBD. Okay, now you bottom-liners can go on and do something else.

The Messy Details

If you've stuck around you must be really short on things to do or terribly interested in the nuances of tax law. In either case, I'm sure we can get together sometime and swap stories of band camp. Following are the details of these two answers, in reverse order (yeah, that'll rock your world!).

125

After RBD

So first let's review RBD: an IRA owner's Required Beginning Date is defined as April 1 of the year following the year in which the IRA owner reaches age 70½. So, if you turn age 70 on or before June 30 of any particular year, your RBD will be April 1 of the following year. If you are first able to refer to yourself as a septuagenarian on or after July 1 of any particular year, your RBD will not occur until April 1 of the second calendar year in the future. For example, if your 70th birthday arrived on July 3, 2012, then you would have an RBD of April 1, 2014.

If the owner of an IRA dies after his or her RBD and there is no designated beneficiary for the account, the rules state that the IRA can be paid out to the heirs or estate over the remaining life expectancy of the original owner. At age 71 (which is the youngest age an IRA owner can be during the year of RBD) the life expectancy table (Table I, Appendix A) indicates a life expectancy of 16.3 years. Since the distributions must begin the year after the IRA owner's passing, the life expectancy would be reduced by 1, resulting in a payout period of 15.3 years. The beneficiary(s) would be determined by an external will, trust, or the courts.

Before RBD

If the IRA owner passed away prior to RBD and there is no designated beneficiary for the account, then the default distribution period is always 5 years. This five years begins with the first year after the former owner of the IRA has passed away. The beneficiary(s) would be determined by a will, applicable trust, or the courts.

38. Disclaiming an Inherited IRA

I know what you're thinking – who would want to disclaim an inheritance, right?

Well, it happens a lot more often than you think – maybe in order to keep from loading one beneficiary's estate with too many assets, or possibly in order to even things out, make it more equal, for all common beneficiaries. So anyhow, the IRS has rules associated with disclaiming an IRA inheritance, and as usual, there is no leeway if you foul it up.

As long as there aren't a lot of extenuating circumstances, a beneficiary disclaiming an inherited IRA is pretty straightforward – spelled out in §2518 of the tax code, as long as the primary beneficiary(s) executes a written instrument to disclaim all or a portion of the inherited IRA within 9 months of the death of the original account owner, the contingent beneficiary(s) will inherit the remaining account.

One additional little wrinkle – the primary beneficiary(s) must not have received a benefit from the account prior to disclaiming. Oh yeah, and one other thing: according to the rules, if the decedent was already subject to Required Minimum Distributions (RMD), the beneficiary must continue those distributions.

If you've been following this, maybe you see the issue: let's say John, the IRA owner, dies in November, and has not taken his RMD for the year. The primary beneficiary, John's daughter Jane, has not had an opportunity to consider whether or not it makes sense to disclaim the inheritance or not, and the year-end is closing fast. So, the RMD is distributed to Jane before the end of the year. According to the rules, Jane has now received a benefit from the account, so she can't disclaim, right?

Taking a required distribution doesn't necessarily make the beneficiary ineligible to disclaim the inheritance. Well, Revenue Ruling 2005-36 clarified, simplified, and made everything square on this issue. Within this ruling, the IRS recognizes sometimes these situations come about, so they've allowed for RMD for the year of death to be distributed to the primary beneficary *but not counted as a benefit for the purpose of disclaiming rule.* So in other words, *the RMD doesn't disqualify the primary beneficiary from having the option of disclaiming.*

In addition, RR 2005-36 clarified a couple of other situations, wherein an primary beneficiary could disclaim a portion of an inherited IRA, allowing the disclaimed portion to flow to the contingent beneficiary(s). This can be done as a specific (pecuniary, to use the IRS' parlance) dollar amount, or a percentage of the account as of the date of death.

The above is important to note, because when a portion of the account is disclaimed, any income attributable to the disclaimed amount has to be disclaimed as well. So if the account was worth $100,000 on the date of death, and the primary beneficiary disclaimed 25%, then the primary beneficiary would receive $75,000 plus the gains or minus the losses associated with the disclaimed portion. The remainder would go to the contingent beneficiary(s). If an RMD is paid to the primary beneficiary and the primary beneficiary later disclaims a portion of the account, the RMD is counted as part of the primary beneficiary's non-disclaimed portion.

39. Spousal Inherited IRA

So far we've discussed inherited IRAs and how to handle them — but we have not covered all of the options for a Spousal Inherited IRA separately. There are some differences, specifically more options available, so this is an important topic. It should be noted, this chapter applies to inheriting IRAs or Qualified Retirement Plans (QRPs, such as a 401(k) or 403(b)), although the term IRA is used throughout. The receiving account must always be an IRA, though.

As a person who has inherited an IRA from your spouse, you have the following options if you are the sole beneficiary of the IRA:

- Leave the IRA where it is, and begin taking distributions based upon your own life (see Table I in Appendix A for the factors). This is the default position.

- Rollover the IRA to an inherited IRA (see Chapter 41 for more information). In this case, you're treating the situation as if you're a non-spouse beneficiary.

- Rollover the IRA into an existing or new IRA *in your own name*. This is the special provision only spouses can use. A non-spouse beneficiary cannot rollover the IRA into an account in his or her own name. (*Note: a spouse beneficiary could also leave the IRA where it is and just begin treating the account as if it was your own — more on this in the next chapter.*)

131

40. Spousal Inherited IRA Rollover

There's nothing terribly complex about the mechanics of a spousal rollover of an inherited IRA – you simply put the paperwork in motion for a rollover, making sure both the original custodian and the new custodian are aware of the fact you're taking advantage of this special provision for spouses. It is also possible to leave the IRA in place where it is and treat the IRA as your own – this will become the default if you 1) make a contribution into the account; or 2) fail to take the RMDs as if the account were inherited.

Now you have the IRA funds in your own account – which you can make contributions to, convert to a Roth IRA, or whatever you'd like. Plus, if you're under age 70½, you don't have to start Required Minimum Distributions (RMDs) from the account. This brings up the one possible downside you should be aware of as well, prompting a word of caution.

A word of caution

IF you go ahead and rollover the IRA from your deceased spouse's account into an account in your own name, if you're less than age 59½, you do not have free access to the funds in the account – one of the 72(t) exceptions must apply (see Chapter 44 later for more details), or you'd be charged the extra 10% penalty in addition to taxes on the withdrawal. It is for this reason many inheriting spouses do not take the IRA on as their own account – especially when there is a potential need to access the funds for income before age 59½. When the IRA is left in the name of the deceased owner, the spouse

133

has the opportunity to withdraw funds from the account at any age without triggering the 10% early withdrawal penalty.

One more provision

As mentioned earlier, the provision for the spousal beneficiary to treat the IRA as her own is generally for a spouse who is the sole beneficiary. There are two ways to resolve this situation if the spouse would like to rollover the account to her own IRA and there is more than one beneficiary.

Other beneficiaries could disclaim the inheritance, leaving only the spouse (see Chapter 38 for more on disclaimers).

Here's an example: Jane, a well-intentioned IRA owner designated her husband Dick and their child Barbie as split beneficiaries of her IRA account. This can bring about unintended results, such Barbie (only ag 9 upon her mother Jane's death) having to take RMDs over a much shorter period than necessary – equivalent to Dick's lifetime. Barbie can disclaim the inheritance and leave only the Dick as a beneficiary. Dick can now set up a new IRA in his own name, with Barbie as the beneficiary of the new account. This will fulfill Jane's original intent, while opening up the account to the extra privileges available to an owner of an IRA versus an inheritant.

A somewhat less messy method is available – as a spousal beneficiary, but not the sole beneficiary, Dick can take a distribution of his entire share from the account, and then roll it over to an IRA in his own name, as long as it's within the 60-day period following the distribution. Dick may need to make up the difference of the withholding if tax has been withheld on the distribution. If Dick doesn't roll over the full amount into his own IRA, he will be taxed and perhaps assessed a 10% penalty on the amount he did not roll into the new account. Using this method eliminates the disclaimer requirement which might be necessary if there are many other beneficiaries or if the other beneficiaries do not wish to disclaim. (*Note: This method is STRICTLY for a spousal beneficiary. A non-spouse beneficiary will bust the stretch IRA by taking a distribution of this type, even if they rollover the amount into a properly-titled account within the time allotted. Those rollovers should ONLY be done via trustee-to-trustee transfer.*)

41. The Non-Spouse Beneficiary

When you inherit an IRA from someone other than your spouse, you are able to take advantage of certain protections or deferrals of tax inherent in the IRA, but you are somewhat restricted in your actions with the account. These rules also apply to a spouse who has elected NOT to treat the inherited IRA as his own IRA.

Restrictions

Specifically, you are not allowed to treat the IRA as your own – in other words, the account can only be re-titled as an inherited IRA. This means you can move the account to another custodian (via trustee-to-trustee transfer only) or leave it at the same custodian, and change the title to read as "John Doe IRA (Deceased January 1, 2009) FBO Janie Brown" or something very similar.

In addition to the restriction on titling, the IRA beneficiary must begin taking Required Minimum Distributions (RMD) as described below:

If the owner of the account died on or after his Required Beginning Date, which is generally April 1 of the year following the year in which he reached age 70½, the RMD is based on the longer of: 1) the owner's life expectancy; 2) the beneficiary's life expectancy; 3) the oldest of multiple beneficiaries' life expectancy (if more than one beneficiary).

If the owner of the account died before his Required Beginning Date, the RMD is based upon the beneficiary's life expectency or the life expectency of the oldest beneficiary if there are more than one beneficiary.

All of the above life expectency references are to be found in Appendix A, Table I.

The Designated Beneficiary

The designated beneficiary is generally determined on September 30 of the year following the year of the death of the plan owner. In order to be named the designated beneficiary, an individual must be named on the plan documents as of the date of death (no changes can be made after death). If any person named in the plan documents as beneficiary is no longer a beneficiary as of September 30 of the year following the year of death, such person will not be considered as a possible designated beneficiary. This could come about if one of the original beneficiaries chose to disclaim entitlement to the account.

If an individual who is the primary beneficiary as of the owner's date of death dies prior to September 30 of the year following the year of death, this individual is still considered to be the primary beneficiary, rather than any contingent beneficiaries. The deceased beneficiary's estate would receive the account and his or her age would be used for determining distribution.

Required Minimum Distribution (RMD) Rules

It is important to note, the following RMD rules apply:

- you're allowed to spread the distribution out in monthly, quarterly, or any schedule of payments as long as it's at least annually;

- if you're the beneficiary of more than one IRA, you must determine the RMD for each IRA individually, although you may total the RMDs and take the amount from a single account if you wish; plus:

- if you receive more than the minimum required in any one year, you do not receive "credit" against future distribution requirements.

Multiple Beneficiaries

If there are multiple beneficiaries of a single account, and all of the beneficiaries are individuals (not trusts), as indicated earlier, the beneficiary with the shortest life expectency (Appendix A, Table I) is used to determine RMD for the account. If an account is split into separate accounts with separate beneficiaries prior to the death of the owner, each account is treated separately with regard to inheritance rules, not aggregated.

Trust as a Beneficiary

If a trust is the named beneficiary, on September 30 of the year following the year of the death of the owner, the beneficiary(s) of the trust will become the designated beneficiary(s) of the IRA as long as the following are true:

- The trust is a valid trust under estate law, or would be but for the fact there is no corpus.

- The trust is irrevocable or will become irrevocable by terms, upon the death of the owner.

- The beneficiary(s) of the trust are specifically identified from the trust document.

- The IRA custodian or trustee has received documentation of the trust by October 31 of the year following the year of the owner's death.

If the beneficiary of the trust is another trust, as long as the second trust meets the requirements above, the beneficiary(s) of the second (or subsequent) trust will become the designated beneficiary(s) of the IRA.

42. Problems Arising From Not Taking Timely Distributions

What happens when a beneficiary doesn't act in a timely fashion with regard to taking Required Minimum Distributions from the inherited IRA?

The Inheritance

So, let's say Jane inherited an IRA from her mother Sylvia – this was Sylvia's own IRA she had contributed to or rolled over funds from a qualified plan at some point, and had designated Jane as the sole primary beneficiary of the account. Things get really hectic and confusing after the death of a parent, and sometimes we don't cover all of the bases properly. In this example, Jane didn't realize she needed to begin taking Required Minimum Distributions (RMD) from her inherited IRA as of December 31 of the year following the year of Sylvia's death.

As of now, for example's sake, let's say we're in the fourth year after Sylvia's passing. *(see Notes below for more info)*

At this point Jane has two choices: take the entire balance of the IRA as a distribution before the end of the fifth year; or "unwind" the mistake by taking the RMDs for the first four years, paying the 50% excess accumulations penalty on each distribution, and then continuing on with her lifetime RMDs. In each case, of course, Jane would be required to pay ordinary income tax on the distributions.

Five Year Distribution

This one is the "default" distribution option — you must take the complete distribution (either a series of payments or a lump sum) within the five years following the year of the original owner's death. In the example we've started, this means Jane has roughly two years to complete this distribution.

Since ordinary income tax is owed on distributions from the inherited IRA, if the balance is significant this could represent a sizeable tax bill. It might even put Jane into a higher (possibly much higher) tax bracket, causing lots of unnecessary additional tax — unless she took the other route.

Unwinding the Mistake

In order to avoid the excess taxes described above in the Five Year Distribution, Jane would need to go back and take distributions for the three prior years she missed, based upon her Table I (Appendix A) factor. For example, let's say Jane's inherited IRA was worth $100,000 at the end of the year in which Sylvia passed away, and Jane's age in the following year was 28. According to Table I, Jane's life expectancy factor is 55.3 years. Dividing the IRA balance by 55.3 gives Jane a Required Minimum Distribution (RMD) of $1,808.32 for the first year.

Unwinding the mistake requires you to catch up on the missed withdrawals and pay the penalties.

Continuing the example, Jane would subtract 1 from her Table I factor of 55.3, and then get the balance of the IRA at the end of the first year minus the RMD from the first year, $1,808.32 - to come up with the RMD for the second year. For the sake of the example we'll assume the IRA is growing at a fixed rate of 5% per year, and so the balance at the end of the second year is $105,000. Subtract $1,808.32 from $105,000 to come up with a year two balance of $103,191.68. Jane's Table I factor is now 54.3 after subtracting 1, yielding an RMD of $1,900.40 ($103,191.68 divided by 54.3 equals $1,900.40).

For the third year, Jane's IRA has grown to $110,250 at the assumed 5% rate. Subtracting her two years' worth of RMD leaves Jane with a balance of $106,541.28, and her Table I factor is 53.3 (just keep subtracting one from the prior year's factor), giving Jane an RMD for the year of $1,998.90.

Adding these three years' worth of RMDs together equals $5,707.62, which Jane would take out in a distribution to make up for the prior years. This amount is subject to ordinary income tax (just like W2 wages), but is also subject to a special tax on "excess accumulation". This tax is for failure to take RMDs in a timely fashion, and amounts to 50% of the missed required distribution.

For the first year, Jane's excess accumulation was $1,808.32, so the excess accumulation tax would be $904.16. For the second year, since she didn't take the RMD for either of the first two years her excess accumulations are $3,708.72, so the tax is $1,854.36. By the third year her excess accumulation is $5,707.62, for an additional tax of $2,853.81. Jane's total excess accumulation tax for the three years is $5,612.33 – nearly as much as the RMDs.

While Jane could take this amount out as an additional distribution, keep in mind she'd have to pay more ordinary income tax on the additional distribution - but at least she wouldn't have to pay the 50% penalty on it. Jane would probably be better off just paying in that amount from the RMDs she's taken to catch up, since she hadn't had that money in her hands anyhow.

For this year, Jane would also need to take a RMD – and continuing our example her IRA balance at the end of last year was $115,762.50 – from which she would subtract the RMDs of $5,707.62, leaving $110,054.88. Jane's Table I factor is 52.3, which provides her with an RMD of $2,104.30, which she needs to take as a distribution by the end of the year. *(Jane will need to continue this RMD calculation process for each year hereafter unless other circumstances change things.)*

Don't Try This At Home, Kids

I know I've cautioned you about this before, and perhaps you see it as a little self-serving (tax guy recommends a tax guy, duh!) but you can really cause yourself some extra grief if you foul this one up. It would be worth it to have a tax professional review your calculations at the very least – and to tell the truth, you're probably just as well to have the tax guy do the calculations for you because the cost is likely about the same for him to review your work as to do it himself. The tax pro can help you with the required filing of Form 5329 (to account for the excess accumulation tax) as well. In addition to the tax, interest may be owed as well on the accumulation tax due in prior years.

Notes:

It should be noted that the fact the decedent is your parent is not critical to the facts of the example above – only that you are inheriting the IRA from someone other than your spouse. A spousal inheritance is a different animal altogether.

A factor of this example that IS important is the IRA belonged specifically to the decedent and is not an inherited IRA. If you've inherited an IRA which was already an inheritance, if it was specifically directed to you as the designated beneficiary then the rules are the same – but if you received the IRA via the estate, you'll have to follow the five-year distribution rule exclusively.

Lastly, it is also important to note the example only identifies a single primary beneficiary – if there is more than one primary beneficiary, the process described would be complicated by the fact that the oldest of all the beneficiaries (with the smallest Table I factor) would be the one whose distribution period is used for all beneficiaries, since the IRA was not split by the end of the year following the year of the death of the original owner. See Chapter 36 for more on splitting an inherited IRA.

43. IRD From an IRA

The topic of Income in Respect of a Decedent (IRD) can be a particularly confusing aspect of the tax code – but it doesn't need to be. Put simply, IRD is any income a decedent would have received had death not occurred – that has NOT been included as income on the final income tax return. In essence, this rule indicaates certain items in the estate, specifically income items, do not receive a step-up in basis. This income has to be accounted for on one of three tax returns:

- estate

- beneficiary

- other assignee (of right to income)

If you are the beneficiary of an IRA and are required to include some IRD on your tax return, you may be eligible for a special IRD deduction. This deduction is limited to any estate tax paid on the income received in respect of the decedent. This would have to be a significant-sized estate, since the applicable exclusion amount for 2012 is $5MM.

It is important to note, the IRD deduction is only certain for federal estate tax – your state estate tax may or may not be deductible.

IRD from an IRA

From an IRA, IRD would include any income you receive that was a portion of the gross estate. Any growth occurring after the date of death of the original owner becomes income to the beneficiary, and therefore is not IRD. Any estate tax attributed to the IRD is deductible as a miscellaneous deduction on Schedule A of Form 1040 – *and this deduction is NOT limited by the 2% floor as are most other miscellaneous deductions.* If the IRA had basis – in other words, if the IRA included non-deductible contributions – then those contributions are not taxed to the beneficiary as IRD. Income tax has already been assessed on those amounts.

Roth IRA Nuances

For a Roth IRA, the IRD would only include income received via non-qualified distributions, and then only the portion representing growth in the account. The main way you could get caught by this one is if the IRA had not been established for the required five-year period prior to the death of the original owner. Any income (growth) in the account up to the date of death is IRD, the contributions are tax-free, and any growth after the date of death is income to the beneficiary.

IRD Deduction

To calculate the IRD deduction, you need to know the amount of the taxable estate, the amount of tax paid on the estate, and the value of the IRD item(s) in the estate. As an example, we'll say we have an estate valued at

$7MM, and an IRA worth $1.5MM. On the entire estate, we paid tax of $700,000.

Next, we calculate the estate tax on the value of the taxable estate without the value of the IRA — and we come up with $175,000. So the estate tax attributable to the IRA is $525,000, or 35% of the IRA value. So, as we take distributions from the IRA, we are allowed to claim a deduction of 35% of each distribution until the entire $525,000 attributed estate tax is used up. This deduction offsets (in theory) the fact you must include the distribution as ordinary taxable income.

Once again, this is not an activity for the faint of heart. I suggest working closely with your tax pro to make sure you're calculating things correctly — it can amount to some sizeable tax issues if you've fouled it up somehow.

Special Weapons and Tactics

Early Withdrawal (72t) Plans

44. Withdraw Retirement Funds Without Penalty (Sec 72t)

Earlier we mentioned there were several exceptions in the Internal Revenue Code (IRC) allowing for an early withdrawal from your IRA or 401(k) without the 10% penalty being imposed. The section of the IRC that explains most of these exceptions is called Section 72(t) (referred to as §72(t) for short), and there are several subsections in this piece of the Code. Each subsection, listed below, has specific circumstances to provide exception to the 10% penalty.

§72(t)(2)(A)(i), (ii), (iii) – age 59½, death, or disability

Three of the most common ways you can withdraw funds from your IRA without penalty are – reaching age 59½, death, and disability.

When you reach age 59½, you can withdraw any amount of your IRA (or other deferred account) without penalty, for any reason. The only thing you have to remember is you must pay ordinary income tax on the amount you withdraw. This means once you have reached the date that is 6 months past your 59th birthday, you are free to make withdrawals from your IRA without penalty.

Upon your death at any age, the beneficiaries of your account or your estate if you have not named a beneficiary, can take distributions from your IRA in any amount for any reason without penalty (and in fact they're required to take distributions).

In addition, if you are deemed "totally and permanently disabled" you are also eligible to withdraw IRA assets for any purpose without penalty. Total and permanent disability means you have been examined by a physician and the disability is such that you cannot work, and the condition is expected to last for at least one year or result in your death.

§72(t)(2)(A)(iv) – series of substantially equal periodic payments (SOSEPP)

This particular section of the Internal Revenue Code – specifically §72(t)(2)(A)(iv) – is the most famous of the 72(t) provisions. This is mostly because it seems to be the ultimate answer to the age-old question "How can I take money out of my IRA early without penalty?"

While it's true this particular code section provides a method for getting at your retirement funds without penalty (and without special circumstances like first-time home purchase or medical issues), this code section is also very complicated. With this complication comes a huge potential for costly mistakes – and the IRS is notorious for NOT forgiving and forgetting!

Early Withdrawal (72t) Plans

In order to set up your Series of Substantially Equal Periodic Payments (SOSEPP), you must use one of the three methods prescribed by the IRS: Required Minimum Distribution method, Fixed Amortization method, and Fixed Annuitization method. (Chapter 45 details these three methods.)

Once chosen, your method cannot be changed under most circumstances. There is one situation providing for a one-time change to your payments, but otherwise the SOSEPP can't be changed. This means every year the SOSEPP is in effect, you must take exactly the amount in your schedule from your IRA, no more and no less. Making a change to your withdrawal schedule will result in your owing the 10% penalty retroactively on all payments received, plus interest. (This is another one of those places where the IRS does not forgive. This is called "busting a SOSEPP".)

In addition, once you've begun your SOSEPP, you must continue the payment schedule until the later of five years or you reach age 59½. Again, this is an area where the IRS doesn't forgive or give any leeway: if you take additional distributions one day before your five years or 59½ birthday is reached, the action will "bust" the SOSEPP, and you'll be liable for 10% penalty on all distributions from your IRA plus interest. Obviously this sort of an arrangement should not be taken lightly, and you must keep excellent, flawless records on your withdrawals.

Other facts about §72(t)(2)(A)(iv):

- You can split your IRA into more than one account, and apply your SOSEPP against only one account, thereby reducing the balance against which your payout method is calculated.

- You can have more than one SOSEPP going at a time, using separate IRA accounts and different payout methods for each.

- Your periodic payment could change under the minimum distribution method, as it recalculates annually based on the account balance at the end of the prior year.

§72(t)(2)(A)(v) – separation from service on or after age 55 (401(k) only)

Did you realize there is a provision within the Internal Revenue Code allowing you to start taking regular distributions from your 401(k) plan *before you reach age 59½?* This little-known section of the code, §72(t)(2)(A)(v), can be a real dandy if you happen to fit the requirements.

Note: although we will refer to the 401(k) throughout this section, this code provision applies to all ERISA-qualified, employer-established defined contribution plans, which includes 401(k), 403(b), 501(a), and others.

Here's how it works: if you are working for a company and are participating in the company's 401(k) plan, should you decide to leave employment at any time during or after the year in which you reach age 55, there will be no penalty for taking distributions from the plan. Normally, any distribution (other than specifically-qualified distributions) prior to age 59½ would result in the 10% penalty being applied.

It is important to note, these distributions only qualify when received from a company-established defined contribution plan – NOT an IRA account. *NUA treatment does not apply to IRAs.* Just to be clear: THIS PROVISION DOES NOT APPLY TO IRA ACCOUNTS. In order to maintain this penalty-free distribution, the funds must not be rolled over into an IRA. This is a critical distinction you need to understand – a mistake would take away this option completely. Make certain you completely understand how this works before starting a distribution, as it could be costly to make a mistake.

Lastly, the Pension Protection Act of 2006 made one additional change to the code: The age limit is reduced to 50 for retiring police, firefighters, and medics - so they can take distributions from their plans penalty-free at age 50 or after, upon leaving employment.

§72(t)(2)(A)(vi) – 404(k) dividends and §72(t)(2)(A)(vii) – levy on a qualified plan

These code sections only apply to non-IRA plans, so we're skipping them for brevity.

§72(t)(2)(B) & (D) – medical expenses, health insurance premiums

There are two different medical purposes allowing for an early, penalty-free withdrawal: high unreimbursed medical expenses and paying the cost of medical insurance. We'll cover these topics separately next.

High Unreimbursed Medical Expenses

If you are faced with high medical expenses for yourself, your spouse, or a qualified dependent, you may be eligible to withdraw some funds from your IRA penalty-free to pay for those expenses. The amount you can withdraw is limited to the actual amount of the medical expenses you paid during the calendar year, minus 7.5% of your Adjusted Gross Income (AGI – the amount on your Form 1040, line 38, or Form 1040A line 22).

You can only count medical expenses that are otherwise deductible on Schedule A of Form 1040 – but you don't have to actually itemize your deductions in order to take advantage of this exception to the 10% penalty.

Medical Insurance Premiums

You may be able to take a penalty-free distribution of some IRA funds to help pay for medical insurance premiums for yourself, your spouse, and your dependents, as long as the amount you withdraw does not exceed the amount you actually paid for medical insurance premiums, and ALL of the following apply:

- You lost your job.

- You received unemployment compensation paid under any federal or state law for 12 consecutive weeks because you lost your job.

- You receive the distributions during either the year you received the unemployment compensation or the following year.

- You receive the distributions no later than 60 days after you have been reemployed.

There is no income limitation on this provision.

Keep in mind, as mentioned previously, these avenues provide a way to withdraw funds from your IRA *penalty-free*, but not *tax-free*. You will still be liable for ordinary income tax on any distributions you take from your deductible IRA.

§72(t)(2)(C) – qualified domestic relations order (QDRO) – upon a divorce settlement (401(k) only)

An exception to the 10% penalty on distributions from a qualified plan (but not an IRA) is when the distribution is pursuant to the imposition of a Qualified Domestic Relations Order, or QDRO (cue-DRO).

A QDRO is often put into place as part of a divorce settlement, especially when one spouse has a considerably larger retirement plan balance than the other. What happens in this case is the court determines what amount (usually a percentage, although it could be a specific dollar amount) of the retirement plan's balance is to be presented to the non-owning spouse. Once the amount is determined and finalized by the court, a QDRO is drafted and provided to the non-owning spouse, which allows the non-owning spouse to direct the retirement plan custodian to distribute the funds in the amount specified.

In the case of a QDRO, the owning spouse will not be taxed or penalized on the distribution. In addition, if the non-owning spouse chooses to rollover the distribution into an IRA, there would be no tax or penalty on the distribution to her, either. If the non-owning spouse chooses to use the funds in any fashion other than rolling over into another qualified plan or IRA, there will be tax on the distribution, but no penalty.

Many times it may make sense for the non-owning spouse to leave the account with the qualified plan (rather than rolling into an IRA) if there may be a need for the funds at some point prior to age 59½. This will be dependent upon just how "divorce friendly" the qualified plan custodian will be.

Of course other 72(t) exceptions could apply, but if there was a need not fitting another exception and the distributee did not wish to establish a series of substantially equal payments for five years, the QDRO would still apply to the distribution from the qualified plan (as long as the funds are still in the plan the QDRO was written to apply to).

As an example, let's say Lester and Edwina (both age 40) are divorcing, and as a part of the divorce settlement, Edwina's 401(k) plan is to be shared with Lester, 50/50, with a QDRO enforcing the split. After a couple of years Lester decides he would like to use some of the funds awarded to him from the divorce to purchase a new fishing boat. As long as the funds are still held in the original 401(k) plan, Lester can request withdrawal and receive the funds without penalty, due to the existence of the QDRO. However, had Lester rolled over the funds into an IRA (or other qualified plan), the QDRO would no longer be in effect, and he would be unable to access the funds without paying the penalty for early withdrawal. *(It is important to note, in either case, Lester would be required to pay ordinary income tax on the distribution.)*

§72(t)(2)(E) – higher education expenses

Another way to pull funds from an IRA or a qualified retirement plan (401(k), 403(b), 457, etc.) without having to pay the 10% penalty is to use those funds for Qualified Higher Education Expenses (QHEE). This comes up quite often, as parents are faced with the issues surrounding the dueling requirements of retirement saving and paying for college for the young 'uns.

In this portion of the code, the provision is made for a qualified retirement plan or IRA owner to withdraw, without penalty, amounts "not to exceed the Qualified Higher Education Expenses for the tax year".

So, you may ask, what is a QHEE? Essentially, this includes tuition, fees, books, supplies, and equipment required for enrollment or attendance at an eligible educational institution. Also included are expenses for special needs services incurred by or for special needs students in connection with their enrollment or attendance.

Room and board also qualifies, but only to the extent it is not greater than the educational institution's allowance for room and board, or the amount the institution actually charges for room and board. In addition, with the passage of the ARRA 2009, computing equipment and services (including internet service) can be included as QHEE.

Who is the student? For the purpose of this provision, the student can be the IRA account owner, her spouse, eligible children (generally dependents), or grandchildren.

Amounts withdrawn must be no more than the QHEE for the tax year, reduced by any additional tax benefits applied: 529 or Coverdell ESA account withdrawals; QHEE covered by HOPE or Lifetime Learning credits; or any grants or scholarships received. If the amount withdrawn is greater than the reduced QHEE, the 10% early withdrawal penalty could be assessed.

§72(t)(2)(F) – first time home purchase

If you are buying, building, or re-building your first home (defined later), you are allowed to take a distribution of up to $10,000 from your IRA to fund a portion of your costs, without paying the 10% penalty. There are a few restrictions, though – here is the official wording from the IRS:

- It must be used to pay qualified acquisition costs (defined later) before the close of the 120th day after the day you received it.

- It must be used to pay qualified acquisition costs for the main home of a first-time homebuyer (defined later) who is any of the following:

    o Yourself.

    o Your spouse.

- Your or your spouse's child.
- Your or your spouse's grandchild.
- Your or your spouse's parent or other ancestor.

- When added to all your prior qualified first-time homebuyer distributions, if any, total qualifying distributions cannot be more than $10,000.

- If both you and your spouse are first-time homebuyers (defined later), each of you can receive distributions up to $10,000 for a first home without having to pay the 10% additional tax.

Qualified acquisition costs. Qualified acquisition costs include the following items.

- Costs of buying, building, or rebuilding a home.

- Any usual or reasonable settlement, financing, or other closing costs.

First-time homebuyer. Generally, you are a first-time homebuyer if you had no present interest in a main home during the 2-year period ending on the date of acquisition of the home which the distribution is being used to buy, build, or rebuild. If you are married, your spouse must also meet this no-ownership requirement.

Date of acquisition. The date of acquisition is the date:

- You enter into a binding contract to buy the main home for which the distribution is being used; or

- The building or rebuilding of the main home for which the distribution is being used begins.

The keys here are to make sure you qualify as a first-time homebuyer (by the IRS' definition above); you use the funds in time (before 120 days has passed); and you haven't taken this option previously. For many folks this can be very helpful in funding the purchase of a home.

Another important point is, although you do not have to pay the 10% penalty on the distribution, you WILL be required to pay ordinary income tax on any money taken from your IRA. This can be a surprise to some folks who weren't expecting it.

45. SOSEPP Distribution Methods

The IRS prescribes three specific distribution methods when utilizing a Series Of Substantially Equal Period Payments, commonly known as a 72t plan or SOSEPP (see more in the previous chapter). The three distribution methods are described here.

RMD Method

The Required Minimum Distribution (RMD) method for calculating your Series of Substantially Equal Periodic Payments (under §72(t)(2)(A)(iv)) calculates the specific amount you must withdraw from your IRA (or other retirement plan) each year, based upon your account balance at the end of the previous year, divided by the life expectancy factor from either Table I (Appendix A) for a single life, Table II (at www.IRS.gov, Publication 590), or Table III (Appendix C, the uniform lifetime table), using the age(s) you have reached (or will reach) for the year. This annual amount will be different each year.

Fixed Amortization Method

Calculating your annual payment under this method requires you to have the balance of your IRA account, from which you then create an amortization schedule over a specified number of years equal to your life expectancy factor from one of the three tables listed above, using the age you have reached (or will reach) for the year, coupled with a rate of interest of your choice - not more than

120% of the federal mid-term rate published by regularly the IRS in an Internal Revenue Bulletin (IRB).

Once you've calculated your annual payment under the Fixed Amortization method, your future payments will be exactly the same until the SOSEPP is no longer in effect. There is a one-time opportunity to change to the Required Minimum Distribution method, described in Chapter 46.

Fixed Annuitization Method

Calculating your annual payment under this method requires you to have the balance of your IRA account and an annuity factor, which is found in Appendix B of Rev. Ruling 2002-62 using the age you have reached (or will reach) for the year, coupled with a rate of interest of your choice - not more than 120% of the federal mid-term rate published by regularly the IRS in an Internal Revenue Bulletin (IRB).

Once you've calculated your annual payment under the Fixed Annuitization method, your future payments will be exactly the same until the SOSEPP is no longer in effect. As with the Fixed Amortization Method, there is also a one-time opportunity to change to the Required Minimum Distribution method, described in the next chapter.

46. One-Time Change to Your SOSEPP

The IRS allows you to change your Series of Substantially Equal Periodic Payments (SOSEPP) allowed under §72(t)(2)(A)(iv) – one time, and only one time. And then, you're only allowed to change your method from either the fixed annuitization method or the fixed amortization method to the Required Minimum Distribution method.

This is the only exception allowed for making a change to your SOSEPP during its enforcement period, which is the later of five years after you started the SOSEPP or when you reach age 59½. The exception is documented in Rev. Ruling 2002-62, 2.03(b). The text of this section of the Revenue Ruling is below.

RR 2002-62 2.03(b)

One-time change to required minimum distribution method. An individual who begins distributions in a year using either the fixed amortization method or the fixed annuitization method may in any subsequent year switch to the required minimum distribution method to determine the payment for the year of the switch and all subsequent years and the change in method will not be treated as a modification within the meaning of § 72(t)(4). Once a change is made under this paragraph, the required minimum distribution method must be followed in all subsequent years. Any subsequent change will be a modification for purposes of § 72(t)(4).

An IRA Owner's Manual

47. Penalties for Changing SOSEPP

So – you've begun your Series of Substantially Equal Periodic Payments (SOSEPP) from your IRA to satisfy your §72(t) requirement. All of a sudden, something happens and you make a change to your payment – either purposely or by accident. What now?

Well – first of all, we must understand the timeline associated with an SOSEPP: once begun (notwithstanding the "one-time change" exception which you can read about in Chapter 46), you have to continue those periodic payments without change for the longer of five years or until you reach age 59½.

If you make a change to your periodic payments (other than the one-time change), §72(t)(4) indicates ALL of your payments, beginning with your first payment under the SOSEPP, will be subject to 1) ordinary income tax (should have already been assessed); 2) the 10% non-qualified withdrawal penalty; and 3) interest on any unpaid tax or penalty, calculated from the date(s) of the disbursal(s) forward to the date you "busted" the SOSEPP.

This is the Code section that should strike the most fear in the hearts of folks who are considering establishing an SOSEPP. If you think about it, the possibilities for error are numerous – your brokerage fails to execute a disbursement the way you directed; you forget to take your withdrawal; you mistakenly take more (or less) than your SOSEPP prescribes. And if it's been in place for several years, you'll owe penalties back to the beginning of the plan, plus interest.

It doesn't take much imagination to envision a scenario where you could be in pretty deep trouble from such an error on your plan. And from what I have experienced, the IRS has very little in terms of a sense of humor when dealing with these cases – not many are overturned.

48. What Happens When Your IRA Runs Out?

What happens when your IRA declines substantially in value and you've put a 72t Series Of Substantially Equal Periodic Payments plan (SOSEPP) into play – and the decline in value has brought your IRA to a point where the balance will no longer support your Equal Payments?

What Happens When Your IRA Will No Longer Support Your SOSEPP?

Here's an example: Dick has set up a SOSEPP in his IRA, beginning at age 50. As we all know (see Chapter 44 for details) Dick has to keep the payments going until he reaches age 59½. Over the course of the years many things can happen, both positive and negative. In this example case, Dick's IRA began with a balance of $100,000, and his annual payments are $3,000. Things go fine for the first few years, although Dick's account doesn't seem to be growing. So, he decides to take a leap and invest it all in a wild-eyed fund – some Madoff fellow's running it. Then, lo and behold, one morning Dick wakes up and find his IRA balance has become – $12 total. Dick is age 56, so he has three and a half more years during which he's supposed to be taking this regular payment of $3,000 from his account! What does he do? He's read about the crazy penalties for busting a 72t payout plan – yikes!

Options

Dick should start by calming down. Taking a deep breath; it's really not so bad. There are a couple of options: He could choose to make the one-time change to his SOSEPP plan. Or, he could choose to let the SOSEPP die, and go on with his life. The best option may be the last one – it allows Dick to be as flexible as possible.

What if Dick decided at this stage he really doesn't need the series of payments anyway? After all, it's just a pain in the rear keeping up with the paperwork and remembering to take the payment each year!

Let it die

If Dick goes ahead and takes the last payment out of his account (the remaining $12) and closes the account – his SOSEPP is no longer in effect. Dick now has the option of starting a new SOSEPP from another IRA account, or just discontinuing the idea of the 72t payout. If he chooses to start a new plan, he'll have to start over with a new five-years.

For SOSEPPs, the IRS considers each IRA separately.

What's key to understand in this is, for SOSEPP's, the IRS considers each IRA account separately – yeah, I know, for everything else, all IRAs are considered as one. What can I say? They don't want you to get too comfortable and start predicting how they'll move – just when you think they're gonna zig? They zag. So with this in mind, if one account (the one with the SOSEPP attached) runs dry, there's no penalty if you just drop it and move on with your life. That's literally all there is to it.

49. How QDRO Impacts SOSEPP

In addition to the 72(t) exception available for folks with a QDRO (Qualified Domestic Relations Order, a court order used to split a 401(k) plan in a divorce), there is also the question of how a QDRO impacts an established Series of Substantially Equal Periodic Payments (SOSEPP) – which, as we know, once established can only be changed one time.

Although not definitive, below are summaries of three Private Letter Rulings (PLRs) which seem to suggest first of all that making the distribution is not subject to the 10% penalty when a QDRO or divorce decree is involved, pursuant to the regulation in Code section 72(t)(4)(A)(ii).

1) The transfer to a taxpayer's spouse pursuant to a divorce decree of 50% of each of three separate IRAs owned by the taxpayer from which the taxpayer had already begun receiving "substantially equal periodic payments" did not result in a modification where the taxpayer's spouse was two years younger and would commence receiving similar payments such that the total of periodic payments to the taxpayer and his spouse subsequent to the division would be substantially equal to the periodic payments received by the taxpayer prior to the division. *PLR 9739044*

2) In PLR 200027060, the IRS rules that a spouse after the divorce who received a portion of the client's IRA accounts which were being used to fund a SEPP, didn't need to continue the payments since it was a transfer

under Code section 408(d)(6). What about the client – did all the payments have to be continued out of what remained of his accounts?

2a) Later in PLR 200050046 (with similar facts) the IRS ruled in favor of the taxpayer.

"*The reduction in the annual distribution from IRA 1 to Taxpayer A beginning in calendar year 2001, prior to Taxpayer A's attaining age 59 1/2, and assuming Taxpayer A has not died and has not become permanently disabled, will not constitute a subsequent modification in his series of periodic payments, as the term "subsequent modification" is used in Code section 72(t)(4), and will not result in the imposition upon Taxpayer A of the 10 percent additional income tax imposed by Code section 72(t)(1) pursuant to Code section 72(t)(4)(A)(ii).*"

In other PLRs, it has further been ruled the IRA owner may reduce the 72(t) payment amount by the same percentage as the reduction in the overall account by distribution to the former spouse. This is the case for a QDRO granting a division of a qualified plan or a divorce decree granting a division of an IRA when the SOSEPP has already been set up. In these cases, the former spouse who *receives* the proceeds from the IRA or qualified plan was not required to continue a 72(t) payment plan – the funds could be rolled over into an IRA, or left in the plan as is.

It is also important to note, the RMD (Required Minimum Distribution) for the year of the transfer is still dependent upon the previous end-of-year balance in the account – and could be adjusted for the following year if a favorable PLR is reached for the case.

Also keep in mind, these PLRs referenced above cannot be used as evidence to back up your own claim. They can help, as referenced, to frame your own requested Private Letter Ruling, but that's all.

Stretching Your IRA

50. A Legacy in the Making

The term "stretch IRA" has become a popular way to refer to an IRA (either Traditional or Roth) which has provisions making it easier to "stretch out" the time funds can stay in the IRA after the death of the owner. A stretch IRA is not a special type of IRA under the Internal Revenue Code, rather, it's a Traditional or Roth IRA which has been passed along to a beneficiary or contingent beneficiary with the option to take distributions over the beneficiary's life expectancy. This arrangement generally allows for successor beneficiaries to be named, facilitating the further tax-deferred growth of the IRA over (possibly) more than one generation. There's nothing really dramatic about this "stretch" activity; any IRA provider can allow it. The fact is, though, many don't. Absent the "stretch" provision, IRA funds might have to be distributed on a much more aggressive basis upon the death of the IRA owner or original beneficiary.

Why Is Stretching an IRA So Important?

Earnings in an IRA grow tax deferred. Over time, this tax-deferred growth can help an individual to accumulate significant funds in her IRA. For someone fortunate enough to have the funds to support herself in retirement without the need to tap into her IRA, continuing this tax-deferred growth for as long as possible may be a priority. Folks in this situation may want for their heirs to benefit from this tax-deferral as well.

An IRA Owner's Manual

As an example, let's say Fred, age 62, has a $400,000 IRA. In addition, having recently retired, Fred has a pension from his former company which pays $40,000 per year, and he has other funds (outside the IRA) providing an additional $15,000 per year in income. Fred's annual living expenses are (conveniently enough for our example) exactly $55,000 per year. With those circumstances, there is no need to withdraw funds from his IRA until he is required to do so (at age 70½). Fred has named his wife Ethel, age 60, as the beneficiary (Fred didn't name her Ethel, her parents named her Ethel – he only named her the beneficiary!). They have agreed, should Fred pass away first, Ethel also would not take distributions from the IRA until required (or necessary), with the intention of leaving the balance of the IRA to their grandchildren. Fred dies at age 70, before reaching age 70½. At this point, the IRA has grown to $687,000 (7% per year). Ethel rolls over the IRA into a new IRA in her name, and does not take a distribution until her age 70½, at which point the IRA has grown to more than $813,000.

Clarifying Two Important Points

Now, a couple of things need to be clear at this point, as the Internal Revenue Code has made this matter quite complicated. The first is, had Ethel been under age 59½ and needed the income from the IRA, she could have begun taking distributions of income from Fred's IRA immediately without penaly – using his attained age rather than her own. Given she did not need the funds, though, it was beneficial for Ethel to rollover the IRA to an IRA in her own name, which allowed for the deferral of the Required Minimum Distribution (RMD) beginning date. It's also important to note, if Fred were the younger of the two, Ethel could have deferred the RMD beginning date until the date Fred would have attained age 70½.

The second point to clarify is when Ethel sets up her rollover IRA, it is critical to specifically name the beneficiaries on the beneficiary form. The reason for this is, upon her death, if the beneficiaries are not specifically named, or if the beneficiaries have pre-deceased the IRA owner and subsequent or contingent beneficiaries are not named on the beneficiary form for the IRA, an entirely new set of rules applies (see Non-Designated Beneficiaries below for this explanation).

By naming the beneficiaries specifically, the intentions of the account owner are clear, and will be carried out as she wished. However – if there is more than one beneficiary, it is important to make sure each beneficiary has had a receiver (rollover) IRA set up and the funds rolled over into the account by the end of the year following the year of death. If these separate accounts have not been established in this timely fashion, the funds must be distributed using the age of the oldest beneficiary as the lifetime. If the accounts are set up as directed though, each beneficiary can use his own age as the lifetime for the distributions.

Meanwhile, Back at the Example...

Continuing our example: Ethel passes away at age 72, having taken two minimum distributions from her account, and the account is now worth over $868,000. She and Fred had named three grandchildren as beneficiaries: Chip, age 30, Robbie, age 20, and Ernie, age 10. (I know I'm off on a tangent here, but they had chosen to disinherit their oldest grandson Mike, since he wasn't around any more after the first season.) Since Ethel had wisely specifically designated the three boys as beneficiaries, each one could establish an inherited IRA and draw out the Required Minimum Distributions using their own ages. For Chip, this means his first distribution would have to be at least $5,431, for Robbie, $4,595, and for Ernie, $3,976. The three boys had had their own separate accounts set up to rollover their inheritances as the law requires. Had they not set up these accounts, all three would have to take distribution of the amount of the oldest beneficiary, Chip. This would mean Robbie and Ernie would be taking unnecessarily large (taxable) distributions from the inheritance.

Another way to deal with this would be to set up a trust as the beneficiary of Ethel's IRA, naming the grandsons as specific beneficiaries of separate trust shares. In this fashion, each would still be able to take distributions over their own lifetimes.

Only a spouse beneficiary may delay taking RMDs.

Bear in mind, these beneficiaries are REQUIRED to begin taking distributions upon their inheritance of the IRA proceeds. The only way to defer taking distributions from an inherited IRA is if the beneficiary is the spouse, which we discussed earlier above. Any other person or trust who is not a spouse must begin taking distributions upon inheriting the IRA, per their own life, using the Single Life table (Appendix A) from the IRS.

Non-Designated Beneficiaries

As mentioned above, if the beneficiary of an IRA is not properly designated on the IRA beneficiary form, a completely different set of rules comes into effect. This situation comes into play when your primary beneficiary pre-deceases you, or if for some reason the original documentation of your beneficiary cannot be found (happens more often than you want to know!). This is why it is critical to make copies of your beneficiary designation form, as well as to check up with your IRA custodian to ensure the proper information is applied to the account. Update these records if your primary or contingent beneficiaries should happen to die before you.

So, if a properly designated beneficiary is not named on the account information, your will (or the state's probate law) will determine the non-designated beneficiary. At this point, if the RMD beginning date for the owner of the IRA has already passed, the beneficiary may take distributions over the remaining life span of the original owner using the Uniform Life table from the IRS. If the RMD beginning date has not passed (in other words, the owner of the IRA is less than age 70½), then the non-designated beneficiary must take distribution of the entire account's proceeds within five years of the end of the year in which the account owner died. Obviously, this is not a preferred method, as all of these distributions are taxable as ordinary income, and this five-year method can result in very large distributions.

Back to our example – had Ethel NOT properly designated her grandsons as beneficiaries and had passed away prior to age 70½, each grandson would be required to take distribution of nearly $290,000 within five years of Ethel's death. Conversely, since Ethel had attained age 70½ by her death, the boys could stretch out their payments over the Uniform Table's (Appendix C) span, amounting to required annual distributions of just a little over $10,000 to each boy, increasing each year until the account is exhausted.

In a nutshell, that's the stretch IRA. It can be pretty complicated, depending upon your wishes, but in most cases it's not too difficult to work out a proper plan. Hopefully the examples have shown the benefit of properly setting up your IRA beneficiaries, as well as making sure your wishes and directions are well understood by your heirs and executor.

51. Mistakes With the Stretch IRA

The stretch IRA, when implemented properly, can be one of the great vehicles for transferring wealth to your heirs, maintaining the tax-deferred status until much later. The problem is, there are some very specific terms which must be met in order to achieve the stretch – and if you screw it up, there's definitely not a *do over* in most of these cases.

Ground Rules

First, let's review the specifics which make up a stretch IRA situation. When an IRA account owner dies, the beneficiary(s) are eligible to re-title the account(s) as inherited IRAs in the name of the deceased owner, and then begin taking Required Minimum Distributions based upon the beneficiary's age – rather than having to take the entire sum all at once and pay tax on it, or the onerous five-year distribution rule which can come into effect if things aren't done properly. (more on the specifics of the Stretch IRA can be found in Chapter 50.)

Keep in mind, these stretch rules apply to both Traditional and Roth IRAs – even though Roth IRA owners are not subject to RMD, their beneficiaries are.

7 Common Mistakes to Avoid

What we're here to discuss are some of the common mistakes often made when attempting to stretch an IRA.

Not properly titling the account – if the account is set up in the name of the non-spouse beneficiary, the funds would be immediately taxable and the IRA would be distributed. There's no remedy to this one, the account has to be titled as "John Doe IRA (Deceased January 1, 2009) FBO Janie Brown" or something very similar.

Doing a "rollover" – while it may seem like an issue of semantics, there is a technical difference between a direct trustee-to-trustee transfer and a rollover. The trustee-to-trustee transfer is self-describing; a rollover is when the beneficiary receives a payment made out in his own name, which he then deposits into an IRA. A rollover is disallowed in attempting to set up a stretch IRA – you must always do a direct trustee-to-trustee transfer.

Neglecting timely transfer – sometimes estates can be tied up for years getting everything sorted out. IRAs and 401(k) plans should not have this sort of problem, as generally there is a specific beneficiary or beneficiaries designated on the account documentation. It is critical to transfer the funds into a properly titled account before the end of the year following the year of the deceased owner's death – otherwise the stretch IRA option is lost, and the funds will have to be paid out via the five year rule.

Failing to take RMD for year of death – if the IRA owner dies after his Required Beginning Date, or RBD, a Required Minimum Distribution must be taken for the year of his death, and cannot be included in a transfer to an inherited IRA. This one can cause some hiccups, but in general can be resolved if caught in a timely fashion by taking the distribution in the name of the decedent and paying the applicable penalties for excess accumulation. If the amount is transferred to the inherited IRA and isn't caught quickly, it could negate the stretch altogether, causing big tax bills.

Missing or neglecting RMD payments – if the beneficiary forgets to take the Required Minimum Distribution payment in a timely fashion, technically the five-year rule could kick in, requiring the entire balance to be paid out within five years, rather than the beneficiary's lifetime. However, it is possible to recover from this mistake, according to the outcome of an IRS Private Letter Ruling (PLR 200811028, 3/14/2008). What happened in this case was the beneficiary neglected to take two years' worth of RMD, and then corrected her mistake in the third year, taking all three years' worth of RMD, followed by paying the penalty (50%) on the missed two years. The IRS ruled the failure to make these distributions in a timely fashion does not make the five year rule apply – and since she maintained the appropriate distributions, caught up on the "misses" and paid the penalties, she is allowed to continue stretching the IRA over her lifetime. *Interestingly, this particular PLR is the first place where the stretch IRA was determined as the default rather than the five-year rule, breaking ground for this to be the case across the board, unless the plan's provisions require the five-year rule.* See Chapter 42 for a more complete explanation of how to resolve the problem of missing timely RMDs.

Not properly designating the beneficiary(s) – IRS regulations state that the beneficiary must be *identifiable* in order to be eligible for the stretch provision. This means naming an individual or individuals as specific beneficiaries on the account forms, or designating a

The beneficiary(s) must be specifically identifiable in order to stretch the IRA.

183

proper "see through" trust (with specific beneficiaries named) as the beneficiary. The account form cannot have something ambiguous like "as stated in will" – since this does not name an identifiable beneficiary. In addition, if the original IRA beneficiary is a trust and *any beneficiary* of the trust is not a person, then the stretch IRA provision is lost for all beneficiaries.

Transferring the balance to a trust – if a qualified "see-through" trust is the beneficiary of the IRA, the balance of the funds in the IRA are NOT transferred to the trust – but rather the IRA is transferred directly to a properly-titled inherited IRA, and then RMDs are taken from the IRA and paid to the trust. According to the trust's provisions, the payments are then made to the trust beneficiary(s). If the payments are simply passed through the trust to the trust beneficiary(s), then each beneficiary will be responsible for any tax on the distribution. If the funds are accumulated in the trust, they are taxable to the trust (to the extent the income exceeds $10,700).

Obviously this isn't an exhaustive list, but rather a sampling of some of the more common sorts of errors folks make when attempting to set up a stretch IRA. Done properly, this sort of arrangement can turn an IRA of a sizeable amount in your lifetime into a very significant legacy to your heirs. Proper setup is very important – get a professional to help you with it if you are confused by how this works!

52. Turn $5,000 a Year Into a $33 Million Legacy

With a headline like that I bet you're thinking this is one of those wild & crazy get rich schemes – which it may be, but it's mostly a demonstration of the great benefit of three factors which can work in your favor in building a legacy:

- compounding interest
- Roth IRA tax laws (including IRA stretch provisions)
- time

What follows is an example of how you can make those three factors work together to create this $33 million legacy.

How It All Started

Once upon a time, there was this guy named Joe. He was 20 years old, working part-time making decent money, finishing up college, just generally living large (by a 20-year-old's definition). On the advice of his father (yes, some 20-year-olds listen to their fathers!), he opened up a Roth IRA, funding it with $5,000. The account was invested in a fixed 5% yield instrument of some sort (it's not important what the investment is, just assume a 5% annual yield).

Using the Roth IRA is advantageous to Joe because his tax rate is very low at this stage of his life – presumably tax rates will be increasing for him in the future. Any growth on this account is tax-deferred and most likely tax-free, as long as any future distributions are for qualified purposes.

Each year thereafter, Joe contributes an additional $5,000 to the Roth account. After he completes college, he starts working at an entry-level job. Not long after, he marries his high school sweetheart Jane, and they settle into their life. As life goes, they soon have children in their household, and even though money is tight, Joe continues to contribute the $5,000 each year into his Roth IRA. This goes on for a while.

And then, 20 years pass

At age 40, Joe launches his own business. During this time in his life, tax deductibility becomes more important to him since he's making a lot more money and is now in a higher tax bracket – and so he stops contributing to the Roth IRA.

All this time, his investments in the Roth account have been steadily growing at the fixed 5% rate – and the balance is now up to $165,329 – on 20 years' worth of $5,000 investments, for a total of $100,000 contributed. Pretty nice, right?

Joe just sets the Roth account aside at this point, forgetting about it altogether for quite a while (other than those pesky quarterly statements). Not much happens here for a long, long time, other than compounding interest, time passing, and continued tax deferral. (Which can have exciting outcomes, as you'll see!)

And another 50 years pass

Joe is now age 90. His business has flourished through the years, now his children are reaping the benefits of having worked there, and are now themselves retiring. His grandchildren have taken over the business, and he and Jane are enjoying their great-grandchildren. A couple of years later, little Jolene is born, and this great-granddaughter quickly becomes the apple of Joe's eye.

It is along this time Joe remembers the long lost Roth IRA account. To this point it has grown to over $2 million – from the original series of $5,000 contributions which amounted to a total of $100,000. Pretty amazing what can happen with compounding interest, right? Now Joe has plenty of other assets he intends to bequeath to his children: the business, other retirement and investment accounts, etc.. This Roth IRA though, he's decided to really make a legacy out of it, and decides to name his great-granddaughter Jolene, a newborn, the primary beneficiary of the account.

And then, a few years later

At age 95, with his family surrounding him, our friend Joe passes away.

Little Jolene is now two years old, and as primary beneficiary of the Roth IRA (now worth over $2.4 million) she must begin taking Required Minimum Distributions from the account, based on her age. Her Table I factor is 80.6, and so her first distribution is for just over $30,000. Her parents file the necessary paperwork and then they put this money away for Jolene's college education fund.

And so on it goes, the account continuing to compound at 5% each year, Jolene receiving her RMD each year, and her parents putting the money away for her college.

Fast forward some more

Little Jolene has graduated from high school, and intends to go off to college. Over the past 16 years since her beloved great-grandpa Joe passed away, she has received a total of over $650,000 in distributions from the Roth IRA he left for her. This has made for a nice start on her college costs. (We won't get into it now, but if we projected college costs out this far into the future, a year of college would cost more than $6 million at the 7% rate of increases we've seen recently.)

So Jolene finishes college, and she continues to receive the RMD payments from the gift from great-grandpa Joe throughout her life. She lives a long, full life, with a loving family and great success. At age 82, according to the original Table I factor, she has depleted the inherited Roth IRA. The total of all of the RMD distributions she received over those 80 years amounts to $33,069,557. Not too shabby for Joe's $5,000-a-year commitment over 20 years.

Note: other than acknowledging they exist, income taxes, inflation, and transfer taxes have not been factored into this example. This example is only intended to demonstrate the value of long-term investing, compounding of interest, and tax-deferral benefits of Roth IRAs, plus the stretch provisions. This example is not intended to represent real life situations, although it is certainly feasible. Bear in mind as well, this entire story took place over the span of approximately 155 years.

Required Minimum Distributions

53. RMD (Required Minimum Distributions)

I've made the observation before – IRAs are like belly-buttons: just about everyone has one these days, and quite often they have more than one. Wait a second, maybe they're not quite like belly-buttons after all. Oh well, you get the point – just about everyone has at least one IRA in their various investment holdings, and these accounts will eventually be subjected to Required Minimum Distributions (RMD) when the owner of the account reaches age 70½.

So what are RMDs, you might ask? When the IRA was developed, it was determined there would be a requirement for the account owner to withdraw the funds which had been hidden from taxes over the lifetime of the account, in order for the IRS to begin benefitting from the taxes levied against the account withdrawals. A schedule was prepared, which approximates the life span of the account owner, and prescribes a minimum withdrawal amount for each year the account owner is alive, until the account is exhausted.

A participant in a Traditional IRA (Roth IRAs are not subject to RMD rules) must begin receiving distributions from the IRA by April 1 of the year following the year the participant turns age 70½. In other words, if the participant reaches age 70 during the months of January through June of 2012, then the participant will reach age 70½ during the 2012 calendar year, so RMDs must begin by April 1, 2013. An individual who reaches age 70 during the latter half (July through December) of 2012 does not reach age 70½ until the 2013 calendar year, and as such, RMDs must begin by April 1, 2014.

After the first year's RMD is taken, the second year's distribution must be taken by December 31 of the same year. In our examples above, the first participant must take an RMD by April 1, 2013, and another by December 31, 2013. The second participant must take an RMD by April 1, 2014 and another by December 31, 2014. For all subsequent years, the RMD must simply be taken by December 31 in order to be credited for the year.

Calculation of the RMD is fairly straightforward, although there is some math involved. For the first year of RMD, if the participant will be age 70, according to the Uniform Lifetime Table (See Appendices A-C for more detail on these tables), the distribution period is 27.4. So if an individual participant has IRAs worth $100,000 at the end of the previous year, dividing the balance of $100,000 by 27.4 produces the result of $3,649.64 – the RMD for the first year. Each subsequent year, you would take the balance of the account(s) on December 31 of the previous year and divide them by the distibution period from the Uniform Lifetime Table, and make sure you take a distribution of at least that amount during the calendar year.

Now, I made a point of indicating that you calculate your RMD based on the balance of *all of your IRAs*. This is because the IRS considers all of your Traditional IRAs as one single account, and you are required to take RMD withdrawals based on the overall total of all accounts. This withdrawal can be from one account or evenly from all accounts, or in whatever combination you wish, as long as you meet the minimum.

Another extremely important point to note: taking these distributions is a requirement. Failing to take the appropriate amount of distribution will result in a penalty of 50% (yes, half!) of the RMD which was not taken. So, as you can see, it really pays to know how to take the proper RMD withdrawals – the IRS has very little sense of humor about it.

Understand the examples I've given are for simple situations, involving the original owner of the account and no other complications. In the case of an inherited IRA or other complicating factors, or if the account is an employer's qualified plan rather than an IRA, many other factors come into play which will change the circumstances considerably. See the earlier chapters on inherited IRAs for more information.

An IRA Owner's Manual

54. Should You Take or Postpone Your First Year's RMD?

As we just discussed, in the first year you're required to start taking Required Minimum Distributions (RMDs) from your IRAs and other retirement plans, you have a decision to make: Should you take the RMD during the first year, or should you delay it to the following year?

The Rule

This decision comes about because of the special rule regarding your first RMD: In the year you achieve age 70½, you don't have to take the first distribution until April 1 of the following year. For each subsequent year thereafter, you're required to take your RMD by December 31 of the year. So this first year provides you with the opportunity to plan the income just a bit.

Generally it's a better idea to take the distribution in the first year, with just a few reasons which might make you reconsider:

- if your income is considerably higher in the first year than it will be in the following year, you might want to delay the distribution, recognizing the income in a year when your tax bracket is hopefully lower. This situation might come about if you've delayed retirement until age 70, so you'd potentially have much more income in the year you were working and then retired, than the following year.

- if taking the distribution would have an adverse impact on your Social Security, causing a higher amount to be taxed in the first year (versus the second year), you might want to delay the distribution.

- other MAGI-limited tax return provisions may impact your decision as well — but these are too varied and specific to the individual to list here

Reasons to NOT Delay

The downside to delaying receipt of the first year's RMD: delaying the distribution to the following year will cause a double-shot of RMD to be recognized as income in the second year. In addition, the two RMDs in one year will be unnecessarily complicated: Each has a different deadline (April 1 for the delayed RMD, December 31 for the *regular* RMD); each is calculated on different account balances (the delayed one is based upon the balance of December 31 of the year before you turned age 70½, the *regular* RMD is based upon the balance one year later); and each is calculated based upon your Table I (see Appendix A) value for different ages (the first is based on your age on your birthday in the first year, the second is based on your age in the second year).

All of these differences add up to lots of confusion and plenty of opportunity for making an error, so unless you have a very compelling reason (such as those listed above) it's probably in your best interest to go ahead and take the first distribution in the first year — when you reach age 70½. *Note: Bear in mind, this planning doesn't apply to inherited IRAs and the RMDs — only to your own regular distributions from your own IRA.*

55. 5 Tactics for Required Minimum Distributions

So – you've reached the magic age, 70½, and now you've got to begin taking the dreaded Required Minimum Distributions (RMDs) from your various retirement accounts. Listed below are a few tactics you might want to employ as you go through this process. Perhaps one or another will make the process a little less onerous on you.

The Tactics

1. Take all of your RMDs from your smallest IRA account. If you have several IRA accounts, you can aggregate the amount of your RMD for the year and take it all out of one (presumably the smallest) account. This way you'll eventually eliminate the extra account, and reduce paperwork, time and error in calculating RMD amounts, as well as complication in estate planning.

The same can be done for your 403(b) accounts - they can be aggregated just like the IRAs. However, you can't use IRA distributions to make up your 403(b) RMDs or vice versa. Each type of account must have its own distributions. This does not apply at all to 401(k) accounts: each 401(k) has its own separate RMD, you can't aggregate the accounts for calculating RMD.

2. Take distributions in kind, rather than in cash. There is no requirement for your RMD to be in cash – so if the situation is advantageous to you, you might consider

taking the distribution in stocks, bonds, or any other investments to fulfill the RMD requirement. When the distribution occurs, the value of the investment is considered taxable income to you – and therefore becomes the new basis of the investment.

There are three situations when this type of distribution is particularly useful:

a) If you wish to remain "fully invested", you will save on commissions since you don't have to sell the investment inside the IRA, remove the cash, and the re-purchase the same investment in your taxable account.

b) If you hold a stock you believe to be undervalued and you expect to appreciate in value, transferring it outside the IRA gives you the ability to receive capital gains treatment on the appreciation. Even better, once outside the IRA, if you hold the stock until your death, your heirs will receive the stepped up basis of the stock as of the date of your death, bypassing tax altogether.

c) If you hold an investment which is particularly difficult to value, such as a thinly-traded stock or a limited partnership, you can take a portion of the distribution from this holding (e.g., if you're required to take 5% of the account, take 5% from the LP and the rest in cash or whatever else the account holds). This way you don't have to sell a portion of the difficult to value holding each year when taking distributions.

3. Take your distribution early in the year. No wait, take it late in the year. There are arguments on either side of the issue, but in general I agree more with the benefit of the latter statement, which I'll explain in a moment.

Taking the distribution early in the year is most helpful for your heirs. If you happen to pass away during the year and have not yet taken the RMD, your heirs will need to make certain the RMD is taken before the end of the year – at a time when they aren't necessarily thinking about this sort of thing.

On the other hand, taking the distribution later in the year provides you with the opportunity to take advantage of any rule changes which Congress tosses your way throughout the year. For example, in 2009 you didn't have to take an RMD at all, and if you did you got to roll exactly one distribution back into your IRA by the end of November. Similarly, in 2006 and again in 2008 and 2010 there were the late-in-the-game rule changes which allowed the IRA holder to make distributions directly to a Qualified Charity, so the income was never factored into the tax return at all (an advantageous thing, especially with regard to Social Security taxation calculations, for example).

So, all in all, I think it's better to wait – at least until the first half of the year is over – before taking the RMD. Besides, your heirs will get over it.

4. Take extra distributions (more than the RMD) when your income is lower. This is similar to the "Fill Out The Bracket" strategy for Roth IRA Conversions (Chapter 26). Essentially you look at your available tax bracket (especially if you are in the lower brackets) and take out extra distributions up to the maximum in your applicable bracket. This will reduce your RMDs in future years, and allow you to either convert those extra funds over to Roth

IRA accounts or a taxable account subject to the much lower capital gains rates.

5. Take extra distributions when subject to AMT. This is mostly useful if you are normally subject to the highest tax brackets (35% these days), but for other reasons you find yourself subject to AMT. You can take additional distributions from your IRA up to the limit that keeps you in the AMT tax, and these funds will only be taxed at a 26-28% rate. These distributions could either be taken as income or converted to a Roth IRA. *(Note: bear in mind, if the final calculation shows you've taken too much from the IRA and kicked yourself back into the 35% bracket, you'll have to work quickly to get the excess rolled back into the IRA account. Extensions of the 60-day rollover period are not allowed in cases like this.)*

Miscellaneous

56. A Cash Flow Dilemma – Should I Take Distributions From My IRA or a Taxable Account?

I know, long title… but I wanted to fully describe the content of this chapter, which is to answer the following dilemma:

I have a sizable IRA and a sizable taxable account holding appreciated stocks. I am in need of additional funds (above any RMD required from the IRA) – so which account should I draw the additional funds from?

Taxable account!

There is one school of thought which says you should take the additional funds from the taxable account, because at today's capital gains rates you will save a bundle in taxes.

The capital gains on your appreciated stock will at most be taxed at 15%, as of this writing. When you compare this tax rate to the ordinary income tax rates, which top out at 35% for 2012 and could rise in the future, this is a bargain. This also assumes you've held the stock for at least 12 months. Otherwise your gains would be taxed at your ordinary income tax rate.

It's a no-brainer, you should always take this extra money from the taxable account, right? No, not always.

IRA account!

There is another school of thought which says, since appreciated stock in a taxable account receives a step-up in basis when inherited, you should leave those funds alone and plan to bequeath them to your heirs at your death. This way the appreciated portion is never taxed.

So when you consider the concept of paying ordinary tax on your IRA distribution and zero tax on the taxable account (assuming you never need to use those funds) versus paying capital gains on the taxable account and potentially leaving your heirs with a fully-taxable IRA (because IRA funds never receive a step-up in basis), this method seems to make a lot of sense.

Conclusion

In the circumstance where you know you're going to need funds from both accounts, it probably doesn't make much difference in the long run, but you would likely come out better using the taxable funds at today's low capital gains rates first. This will hold true until changes are made to the capital gains tax rates which might make this method less desirable.

But if your holdings are large enough in either account to cover your needs for the long term, with some planning of your distributions you might come out better with the second method. Or rather, your heirs will come out better in the long run, due to the basis step-up.

57. How QDRO Impacts NUA

Don't let the alphabet soup in the title put you off. If you've never come face-to-face with a QDRO you might not need to know this — but then again, the basic underlying premises are good information to understand...

First some definitions, just so we know what we're talking about:

QDRO: Qualified Domestic Relations Order — this is a method for permitting distributions from a qualified retirement plan (not an IRA) in the event of a divorce. What happens is, upon the court-decreed division of assets, if the retirement plan (such as a 401(k) or 403(b)) of one spouse is chosen as an asset to be divided and a portion given to the other spouse, then a QDRO, which is a court order, is issued. This QDRO allows the division to occur without penalty. Otherwise, making a distribution from a qualified plan before age 59½ would result in penalty and possible taxation, as we all know. The QDRO provides a way for the receiving spouse to rollover the funds into an IRA of his or her own, without tax or penalty to either spouse.

NUA: Net Unrealized Appreciation — this is a special provision from qualified retirement plans which allows the employee to elect to treat company stock differently from all other assets in the plan when making a distribution from the plan. Essentially, you can pay ordinary income tax on the basis of the stock in your employer's (actually former employer's) company, and then place the stock in a taxable brokerage account, making any gains on the stock

A QDRO doesn't automatically disqualify the account owners from using NUA treatment. subject only to capital gains tax (rather than ordinary income tax, which could be much greater). The trick is, you can only do this maneuver one time, and the distribution must be in a lump sum of all your 401(k) account holdings. Everything in the account which is not company stock to be treated with NUA can be rolled over into an IRA and maintain tax deferral as usual. It's critical to note, this can be the only year you take distribution of funds from the account – if you were to rollover a small amount of funds in a previous year, you can no longer take advantage of the NUA provision (see Chapter 20 for more on NUA).

QDRO and NUA

So the question comes up – if a QDRO distribution occurs for your account, and the distribution includes company stock: does this "bust" the employee's ability to later have the company stock treated with the NUA privilege, since the rule states the distribution must be a one-time single lump-sum distribution?

(drum roll...) The answer is NO. A QDRO is a division of the account, and though technically a distribution has occurred, this distribution does not impact the remaining account's ability to take advantage of the NUA provision. The employee can go ahead and, upon separation from service, perform the lump-sum distribution of the stock and rollover the remainder into an IRA and get the NUA treatment for the stock.

Now, if you're really astute, the last paragraph made you think of another question *(it's okay to admit it if you aren't tax-geeky enough to have thought of this question)*: Can the ex-spouse (the one receiving a split of the employee's plan) elect NUA treatment of any stock which was included in his portion of the account?

(drum roll...) The answer is a qualified YES. The qualification is this: As long as the rest of the account is eligible to be distributed to include NUA treatment, the QDRO'd portion of the account can also take advantage of this provision.

In other words, although the ex-spouse of the employee could roll over the QDRO'd qualified retirement plan into an IRA at any time, if the account contains appreciated employer stock (stock of the former spouse's employer) – it may be in the best interest of the receiving spouse to wait until the employee reaches age 59½ or leaves employment (termination or retirement), so he or she can take advantage of the NUA provision. Otherwise, any rollover will squash this option forever.

Example

Here's a quick example to illustrate: Dick and Jane are divorcing. Dick has a 401(k) plan with his employer, including some stock in his employer's company. Part of the divorce includes a QDRO to give Jane half of the 401(k) plan.

Once the QDRO is completed, Dick still has his original 401(k) account (albeit diminished by half), and Jane has an account in the plan of equal size. Jane can rollover those funds into an IRA at any time, if she chooses, without penalty. However, since the account holds highly appreciated company stock, in order to qualify for NUA treatment, she must maintain the account in the 401(k) plan until Dick terminates employment, retires, or reaches age 59½. At that time, she can pull the lump-sum distribution for NUA treatment and rollover the rest into an IRA. Dick can elect NUA treatment for his account when he terminates employment or retires.

58. Turns Out You Can Be a Little Bit Pregnant

Remember back in junior high during health class (or sex ed, or whatever they called it where you went to school) – it was explained that pregnancy is a black or white thing; "nobody gets just a little bit pregnant" was the story my health teacher gave us to remember. As it turns out, there are many other absolutes in life which are similar. However, in a totally characteristic move, the IRS gives us a way to take something that you would think would be absolute, and twist it so you can, in fact, be a little bit pregnant (or rather, a little bit taxable, a little bit tax free, in this case).

Confused yet? Sorry, that wasn't my intent. Some people refer to this as the "cream in the coffee" rule – meaning, you can't take out only the coffee once cream has been added, you have to take out both cream and coffee. I also like to think of this as the Donny & Marie rule – you remember, "I'm a little bit country. I'm a little bit rock and roll"? Oh, for pete's sake, enough with the analogies! Let's get into this.

IRA Funds – Part Taxable, Part Tax-Free

If you have made after-tax contributions to your IRA, you are likely expecting to at some point take those contributions out again, tax free. And you're right to expect that, because it's exactly what you can do. However (and always a however in life, right?), if the after-tax money you have in your IRA isn't the only money in ALL of your IRAs, any money you take out will be partly taxable and partly tax-free (this was where the "little bit pregnant" thing comes in).

Here's how it works: for example, let's say Jack has two IRAs, each worth $5,000. One is a Traditional deducted (pre-tax) IRA, and the other is a Traditional non-deducted (after-tax) IRA. If Jack wanted to take $100 out of either account, *the IRS considers all of Jack's IRAs as one* – and money taken out of the account(s) comes out ratably. So when Jack takes $100 out of either account, $50 will be tax-free, and $50 will be taxed.

Let's do another example, a little more real world: Jill has two IRAs, one worth $5,000, which is made up of a $3,000 deducted contribution and $2,000 worth of growth and interest; and the second is made up of a $4,000 deducted contribution, a $5,000 non-deducted contribution, and $1,000 worth of growth and interest, for a total of $10,000. Jill would like to take a distribution of $1,500 from one of the accounts. In the IRS' eyes, Jill is taking out $500 which is non-taxed, and $1,000 which will be taxed. This is because, out of the total of $15,000 in the two accounts, only $5,000 was "after tax" funds. Everything else, the growth and interest and the deductible contributions, is considered taxable.

How To Get Around It (or How You Can NOT Be A Little Bit Pregnant)

Don't lose faith, though. There is one way around this dilemma. The IRS allows you to roll over funds from your IRA into a Qualified Retirement Plan (QRP) such as a 401(k) plan – but ONLY the taxable portion, if there are commingled funds in your account(s). So, in this case, the

IRS goes along with the absolute (go figger – they treat the same money two different ways!) and allows no after-tax contributions to be rolled over into a QRP.

So, if Jill has a 401(k) plan at work, or an existing 401(k) which she hasn't rolled over into an IRA, she can use this account to split out her taxable IRA money from the non-taxable IRA money. And then she could do a tax-free conversion of the non-taxed IRA money into a Roth IRA if she wished, for example, as long as she fit all the other criteria. Jill could also simply withdraw the after-tax funds (all she has left in the IRAs now) without tax.

An IRA Owner's Manual

59. Using Your IRA to Reduce or Eliminate Quarterly Estimated Tax Payments

Retirees: don't you get tired of making those quarterly tax payments? January, April, June and September, like clockwork, you have to hand over tax money, just because you're receiving a pension, retirement funds, and/or Social Security benefits. What if there was a way to send this money off one time, and then you wouldn't have to remember it every few months?

There is.

IRA Trick – Eliminating Quarterly Estimated Tax Payments

A little-known fact about IRA distributions is when you have taxes withheld from the distribution (which are then sent directly to the IRS), the withheld money is considered to have been received throughout the year – even if it is received late in December. Using this fact to your advantage, you could figure out how much your total estimated tax payments should be for the year sometime in early December, and then take a distribution from your IRA of amount of your tax calculation. Here's the trick: Instead of taking the distribution yourself, fill out a form W-4P to direct the funds to be withheld and sent to the IRS. Voila! You've now made even payments to the IRS for each of the four quarters, on time with no penalties!

The downside to this plan is, in the event of the taxpayer's untimely death before the annual distribution is made, the estimated payments will be considered as unpaid

209

up to the date of death, and therefore the estate will be responsible for paying the underpayment penalty. Other than that shortcoming, this trick could provide you with several months' additional interest/return on your money, plus remove the hassle of the quarterly filings.

But, Jim, what if I'm retired and under age 59½? Won't there be a penalty?

There doesn't have to be, although I'd place this particular move into the "higher degree of difficulty" category of tricks – not to be taken lightly.

Pre-59½ Retiree: How to Avoid Penalty?

Same situation as before, but now you must take another step: once you've taken the distribution and properly filed the W-4P to have the distribution withheld as tax – execute a 60-day rollover, placing the same amount of money either into the same IRA or another IRA. Effectively, you've pulled the old switcheroo with the IRS on this: What has happened is you've paid tax with a distribution that didn't happen!

You can use your IRA to make your tax payments without penalty. How can this be? Well, the IRS allows you to replace (or rollover) money from any source back into your IRA, so it doesn't matter that your original distribution was used for withholding. So you have made up for missing all those quarterly estimated payments (no underpayment penalty now) plus by rolling over the funds you've avoided the 10% early withdrawal penalty as well.

Caveat

I mentioned that this last trick fits into the "higher degree of difficulty" category of tricks. The reason I say this is because using your account in this fashion (essentially a 60-day loan) can be hazardous – the primary reason: 60 days is all you have, and 60 days can be a relatively short period of time. Plus, the IRS HAS NO SENSE OF HUMOR ABOUT THIS. If you miss the rollover period by one day, you're outta luck.

In addition to the 60-day period, there is also the limitation of only one 60-day rollover per 12-month period (see Chapter 19 for more). Again, remember: no sense of humor at the Service. This is especially true if it's clear you've been pulling a fast one on them with a scheme like I have suggested above. It is for these reasons this rollover trick should only be used in the most dire of circumstances – such as if you completely forgot to make quarterly payments and are facing a stiff underpayment penalty, for example. Otherwise, I'd suggest leaving this one alone. By all means, you should not try this trick year after year.

An IRA Owner's Manual

60. Deducting IRA Losses

Did you know you could deduct losses in your IRA accounts? It's not as simple as it sounds... but it is available and can be a sort of consolation prize for the poor individual who fits the circumstances.

Deducting Losses on a Traditional IRA

Of course, in order to deduct a loss, you have to have a basis in the account, since by definition a loss results when your balance is less than the basis. The only way to have a basis in a Traditional IRA is to have non-deductible contributions in the account. In other words, contributions you made but did not deduct from your income for tax purposes.

If your Traditional IRAs have experienced significant losses (with respect to the basis), you have the option to claim the loss as a miscellaneous itemized deduction on your Schedule A, subject to a 2% of AGI floor.

For example, if Dick had IRAs with a basis of $5,000 and his investments had lost value to a point where the account was worth $100, Dick has a loss of $4,900. For our example we'll say Dick has a household AGI of $75,000. He is eligible to deduct $3,400 as a miscellaneous itemized deduction – his loss is $4,900 and the 2% AGI floor is $1,500, so the difference, the deduction, is $3,400.

In order to do this, Dick's loss must be across all of his IRAs aggregated, and he must close ALL of his Traditional IRA accounts and take distribution of all funds

213

from those accounts. In other words, if Dick has a loss in one account and a gain in another account, his loss has to be netted with all accounts aggregated in order to take advantage of this deduction.

Deducting Losses on a Roth IRA

The same holds for a Roth IRA – but you always have basis in a Roth, since by definition all contributions or conversions constitute basis in the account. The same rule applies here though: you must close ALL Roth accounts and take distribution of the funds in order to take this deduction, and the loss must be an overall net loss considering all of your Roth accounts in aggregate.

In some cases you might be able to isolate a loss in your IRAs via conversions, rollovers or recharacterizations. In general, this deduction is a last-ditch effort for situations where things have really gone south in your accounts. As mentioned before, it can be pretty hairy to work out the details, but it can also be a "consolation prize" if you've found yourself in this position.

61. The Self-Directed IRA

In theory, the description "Self-Directed" applies to most all IRAs. For instance, Wikipedia defines a Self-Directed IRA as follows:

A Self-Directed Individual Retirement Arrangement is an IRA that requires the account owner to make investment decisions and investments on behalf of the retirement plan. IRS regulations require that either a qualified trustee, or custodian hold the IRA assets on behalf of the IRA owner. Generally the trustee/custodian will maintain the assets and all transaction and other records pertaining to them, file required IRS reports, issue client statements, assist in helping clients understand the rules and regulations pertaining to certain prohibited transactions, and perform other administrative duties on behalf of the Self-directed IRA owner for the life of the IRA account. The custodian usually offers a selection of standard asset types that the account owner can select to invest in, such as stocks, bonds, and mutual funds. In addition, most custodians will also permit the account owner to make other types of investments. The range of permissible investments is broad, however, the IRS does place limits on the types of assets that may be invested in and on the types of transactions that may be carried out.

This is a broad description of most IRAs in use today. In practice though, and in fact throughout most of the financial industry, the term "Self-Directed" refers to an IRA which invests primarily in non-traditional sorts of assets. For example, you would use a Self-Directed IRA to invest directly in real estate property, as opposed to stocks, bonds, or mutual funds (considered "common" IRA investments).

So, if you are looking to invest in real estate, non-public limited partnerships, or non-publicly-traded corporations, the typical IRA custodians (mutual fund companies, brokerages, banks, etc.) will not be able to manage your account adequately. Most often you'll find these non-traditional investments are not available at all via those custodians. What you'll need is a custodian who specializes in the type of investment you're hoping to make.

Specialized IRA Custodians

There are many specialized IRA custodians out there in the marketplace who can help with investment in real estate and other investments. (Just do a Google search of "Self-Directed IRA custodian" for an extensive list.) These custodians are able to assist in the overall process of purchasing, managing, and handling the paperwork with the IRS for these investments. The reason you need a specialist is because these non-traditional investments have characteristics which could cause issues with the IRS if not handled appropriately. A few of these characteristics are listed below:

Unrelated Business Taxable Income (UBTI) - If an investment produces income which is "not exempt" from tax, there could be Unrelated Business Income Tax (UBIT) applied. This may sound strange, as you have probably always believed investment income within an IRA isn't taxed until withdrawn - but UBTI is an exception. The key here is the "not exempt" attribute, which refers generally to income *derived from debt-financing and/or unrelated business*. Dividends, royalties, and rent are "exempt" income, as are capital gains. Real estate, limited partnerships and small (non-public) corporations often have UBTI as a matter of normal business activity. And if you own a business entity via your IRA which produces UBTI, you'll need to handle it appropriately. This can include filing a Form 990T tax return to pay the UBIT. A specialist custodian will assist with properly filing the return and paying the tax - which must come from the IRA's assets, not from outside funds.

Don't take this to mean that real estate should never be a part of your IRA investments – in fact, it can be a very good choice in some real estate climates. The primary caution here is with investing in real estate using debt financing.

Indirect Benefit - Many self-directed IRAs eventually face this issue. For example, you may own a rental property and wish to spend your vacation there. Other indirect benefits include paying yourself (or your company) to do work for the company or property owned by the IRA; lending money to or from the IRA; and purchasing property that you or your family will use (such as a vacation or retirement home). These types of transactions are forbidden, and a specialized custodian will be able to help you navigate through without making a mistake.

Self-Dealing - As with the Indirect Benefit issue, many self-directed IRAs confront the issue of self-dealing. This is described more completely in Chapter 8, but the gist of it is you and your family can't buy from or sell to your IRA, or borrow money from the IRA, among other activities. Again, a specialized custodian will assist in making sure these sorts of transactions don't occur.

Appendices

Appendix A

Table I
(Single Life Expectancy)
(For Use by Beneficiaries)

Age	Life Expectancy	Age	Life Expectancy
0	82.4	28	55.3
1	81.6	29	54.3
2	80.6	30	53.3
3	79.7	31	52.4
4	78.7	32	51.4
5	77.7	33	50.4
6	76.7	34	49.4
7	75.8	35	48.5
8	74.8	36	47.5
9	73.8	37	46.5
10	72.8	38	45.6
11	71.8	39	44.6
12	70.8	40	43.6
13	69.9	41	42.7
14	68.9	42	41.7
15	67.9	43	40.7
16	66.9	44	39.8
17	66.0	45	38.8
18	65.0	46	37.9
19	64.0	47	37.0
20	63.0	48	36.0
21	62.1	49	35.1
22	61.1	50	34.2
23	60.1	51	33.3
24	59.1	52	32.3
25	58.2	53	31.4
26	57.2	54	30.5
27	56.2	55	29.6

Table I
(Single Life Expectancy)
(For Use by Beneficiaries)

Age	Life Expectancy	Age	Life Expectancy
56	28.7	84	8.1
57	27.9	85	7.6
58	27.0	86	7.1
59	26.1	87	6.7
60	25.2	88	6.3
61	24.4	89	5.9
62	23.5	90	5.5
63	22.7	91	5.2
64	21.8	92	4.9
65	21.0	93	4.6
66	20.2	94	4.3
67	19.4	95	4.1
68	18.6	96	3.8
69	17.8	97	3.6
70	17.0	98	3.4
71	16.3	99	3.1
72	15.5	100	2.9
73	14.8	101	2.7
74	14.1	102	2.5
75	13.4	103	2.3
76	12.7	104	2.1
77	12.1	105	1.9
78	11.4	106	1.7
79	10.8	107	1.5
80	10.2	108	1.4
81	9.7	109	1.2
82	9.1	110	1.1
83	8.6	111 and over	1.0

Source: IRS Publication 590

Appendix B

IRS Table II is too large to recreate here. Table II, also known as the Joint and Last Survivor Expectency Table, is for use by IRA owners whose spouses are more than 10 years younger and who are the sole beneficiaries of the IRA account. You can find Table II in the appendix for Publication 590, at www.IRS.gov.

Appendix C

Table III
(Uniform Lifetime)

For Use by:

- Unmarried Owners,
- Married Owners Whose Spouses Are Not More Than 10 Years Younger, and
- Married Owners Whose Spouses Are Not the Sole Beneficiaries of Their IRAs

Age	Distribution Period	Age	Distribution Period
70	27.4	93	9.6
71	26.5	94	9.1
72	25.6	95	8.6
73	24.7	96	8.1
74	23.8	97	7.6
75	22.9	98	7.1
76	22.0	99	6.7
77	21.2	100	6.3
78	20.3	101	5.9
79	19.5	102	5.5
80	18.7	103	5.2
81	17.9	104	4.9
82	17.1	105	4.5
83	16.3	106	4.2
84	15.5	107	3.9
85	14.8	108	3.7
86	14.1	109	3.4
87	13.4	110	3.1
88	12.7	111	2.9
89	12.0	112	2.6
90	11.4	113	2.4
91	10.8	114	2.1
92	10.2	115 and over	1.9

Source: IRS Publication 590

Appendix D
MAGI Limits

Listed below are the MAGI limits for the tax year 2012 for the three separate filing status groups –

1. Married Filing Jointly or Qualifying Widow(er);

2. Single or Head of Household; and

3. Married Filing Separately.

2012 MAGI for Married Filing Jointly or Qualifying Widow(er)

Note: for the purposes of IRA MAGI qualification, a person filing as Married Filing Separately, who did not live with his or her spouse during the tax year, is considered Single and will use the information in that section to determine eligibility.

For a Traditional IRA

If you are not covered by a retirement plan at your job and your spouse is not covered by a retirement plan, there is no MAGI limitation on your deductible contributions.

If you are covered by a retirement plan at work, and your MAGI is $92,000 or less, there is also no limitation on your deductible contributions to a Traditional IRA.

If you are covered by a retirement plan at your job and your MAGI is more than $92,000 but less than $112,000, you are entitled to a partial deduction, reduced by 25% for every dollar over the lower limit (or 30% if over age 50), and rounded up to the nearest $10. If the amount works out to less than $200, you are allowed to contribute at least $200.

If you are covered by a retirement plan at your job and your MAGI is more than $112,000, you are not entitled to deduct any of your Traditional IRA contributions for tax year 2012. You are eligible to make non-deductible contributions, up the annual limit, and those contributions can benefit from the tax-free growth inherent in the IRA account.

If you are not covered by a retirement plan at your job, but your spouse IS covered by a retirement plan, and your MAGI is less than $173,000, you can deduct the full amount of your IRA contributions.

If you are not covered by a retirement plan but your spouse is, and your MAGI is greater than $173,000 but less than $183,000, you are entitled to a partial deduction, reduced by 50% for every dollar over the lower limit (or 60% if over age 50), and rounded up to the nearest $10. If the amount works out to less than $200, you are allowed to contribute at least $200.

Finally, if you are not covered by a retirement plan but your spouse is, and your MAGI is greater than $183,000, you are not entitled to deduct any of your Traditional IRA contributions for tax year 2012. You are eligible to make non-deductible contributions, up the annual limit, and those contributions can benefit from the tax-free growth inherent in the IRA account.

Miscellaneous

<u>For a Roth IRA</u>

If your MAGI is less than $173,000, you are eligible to contribute the entire amount to a Roth IRA.

If your MAGI is between $173,000 and $183,000, your contribution to a Roth IRA is reduced ratably by every dollar above the lower end of the range, rounded up to the nearest $10. If the amount works out to less than $200, you are allowed to contribute at least $200.

If your MAGI is $183,000 or more, you cannot contribute to a Roth IRA.

2012 MAGI Limits for Single or Head of Household

Note: for the purposes of IRA MAGI qualification, a person filing as Married Filing Separately who did not live with his or her spouse during the tax year, is considered Single and will use the information in this section to determine eligibility.

<u>For a Traditional IRA</u>

If you are not covered by a retirement plan at your job, there is no MAGI limitation on your deductible contributions.

If you are covered by a retirement plan at work, if your MAGI is $58,000 or less, there is also no limitation on your deductible contributions to a Traditional IRA.

If you are covered by a retirement plan at your job and your MAGI is more than $58,000 but less than $68,000, you are entitled to a partial deduction, reduced by 50% for every dollar over the lower limit (or 60% if over age 50), and rounded up to the nearest $10. If the amount works out to less than $200, you are allowed to contribute at least $200.

If you are covered by a retirement plan at your job and your MAGI is more than $68,000, you are not entitled to deduct any of your Traditional IRA contributions for tax year 2012. You are eligible to make non-deductible contributions, up the annual limit, and those contributions can benefit from the tax-free growth inherent in the IRA account.

For a Roth IRA

If your MAGI is less than $110,000, you are eligible to contribute the entire amount to a Roth IRA.

If your MAGI is between $110,000 and $125,000, your contribution to a Roth IRA is reduced ratably by every dollar above the lower end of the range, rounded up to the nearest $10. If the amount works out to less than $200, you are allowed to contribute at least $200. If your MAGI is $125,000 or more, you cannot contribute to a Roth IRA.

2012 MAGI Limits for Married Filing Separately

Note: for the purposes of IRA MAGI qualification, a person filing as Married Filing Separately, who did not live with his or her spouse during the tax year, is considered Single and will use the information in that section to determine eligibility.

Miscellaneous

For a Traditional IRA

If you are not covered by a retirement plan at your job and your spouse is not covered by a retirement plan, there is no MAGI limitation on your deductible contributions.

If you are covered by a retirement plan at your job and your MAGI is less than $10,000, you are entitled to a partial deduction, reduced by 50% for every dollar (or 60% if over age 50), and rounded up to the nearest $10. If the amount works out to less than $200, you are allowed to contribute at least $200.

If you are covered by a retirement plan at your job and your MAGI is more than $10,000, you are not entitled to deduct any of your Traditional IRA contributions for tax year 2012. You are eligible to make non-deductible contributions, up the annual limit, and those contributions can benefit from the tax-free growth inherent in the IRA account.

If you are not covered by a retirement plan but your spouse is, and your MAGI is less than $10,000, you are entitled to a partial deduction, reduced by 50% for every dollar over the lower limit (or 60% if over age 50), and rounded up to the nearest $10. If the amount works out to less than $200, you are allowed to contribute at least $200.

Finally, if you are not covered by a retirement plan but your spouse is, and your MAGI is greater than $10,000, you are not entitled to deduct any of your Traditional IRA contributions for tax year 2012. You are eligible to make non-deductible contributions, up the annual limit, and those contributions can benefit from the tax-free growth inherent in the IRA account.

For a Roth IRA

If your MAGI is less than $10,000, your contribution to a Roth IRA is reduced ratably by every dollar, rounded up to the nearest $10. If the amount works out to less than $200, you are allowed to contribute at least $200.

If your MAGI is $10,000 or more, you can not contribute to a Roth IRA.

Acronyms

CODA – Cash Or Deferred Arrangement (a QRP)

ERISA – Employee Retirement and Income Security Act

FBO – For the Benefit Of – a way of titling an IRA account

IRA – Individual Retirement Arrangement

OPY – One-(rollover)-Per-Year rule

QRP – Qualified Retirement Plan

RBD – Required Beginning Date (April 1 of the year following the year the IRA owner reaches age 70½)

RIRA – Roth IRA

RMD – Required Minimum Distribution

TIRA – Traditional IRA

TTT – Trustee-To-Trustee transfer

UBIT – Unrelated Business Income Tax

UBTI – Unrelated Business Taxable Income

Index

aggregation rules, *93*
band camp, *125*
busting a SOSEPP, *153*
Collectibles, *27*
designated beneficiary, *138*
disqualified person, *27*
Distribution Ordering Rules, *92*
Employee Retirement Income Security Act, *1*
ERISA, *1*
excess accumulations, *141*
Fixed Amortization Method, *163*
Fixed Annuitization Method, *164*
Form 5329, *144*
HEART Act, *119*
Heroes Act, *119*
Income in Respect of a Decedent, *147*
IRD, *147*
life insurance, *28*
MAGI, *15*
Modified Adjusted Gross Income, *15*
Net Unrealized Appreciation, *71*
non-spouse beneficiary, *63*
NUA, *71, 201*
One-Rollover-Per-Year, *65*
One-Time Change to Your SOSEPP, *165*
Order of Contributions, *21*
order of distribution, *92*
Per Capita, *13*
Per Stirpes, *13*
Prohibited Transactions, *27*
provisional income, *99*
QDRO, *157, 171, 201*
QHEE, *159*
Qualified Domestic Relations Order, *157*
Qualified Higher Education Expenses, *159*
RBD, *125*
Required Beginning Date, *125*
Rev. Ruling 2002-62, *165*
RMD Method, *163*
Self-Directed, *215*
Series of Substantially Equal Periodic Payments, *153*
Servicemember's Group Life Insurance, *119*
SGLI, *119*
SOSEPP, *153*
stretch IRA, *175*
Trustee-to-Trustee Transfer, *62*
UBTI, *216*
Unrelated Business Taxable Income, *216*
unwind, *141*

Made in the USA
San Bernardino, CA
09 December 2013